LIFE TOGETHER STUDENT EDITION

SHARING

YOUR STORY AND GOD'S STORY

LIFE TOGETHER STUDENT EDITION

SHARING

YOUR STORY AND GOD'S STORY

6 small group sessions
on evangelism

Doug Fields &
Brett Eastman

SHARING Your Story and God's Story: 6 Small Group Sessions on Evangelism

Youth Specialties Books, 300 South Pierce Street, El Cajon CA 92020, are published by Zondervan, 5300 Patterson Avenue Southeast, Grand Rapids MI 49530

Library of Congress Cataloging-in-Publication Data

Fields, Doug, 1962-
  Sharing your story and God's story : 6 small group sessions on
evangelism / by Doug Fields and Brett Eastman.
        p. cm.
Summary: Presents lessons to be used by small groups to explore ways to
share faith in Jesus through prayer, scripture, fellowship, and
ministry.
  ISBN 0-310-25337-3 (pbk.)
  1. Christian teenagers--Religious life--Juvenile literature. 2.
Evangelistic work--Juvenile literature. [1. Witness bearing
(Christianity) 2. Christian life. 3. Teenagers--Religious life.] I.
Eastman, Brett, 1959- II. Title.
  BV4531.3.F544 2005
  259'.23--dc21

                          2003005875

Concept and portions of this curriculum are from Doing Life Together (Zondervan, 2002), used by permission from Brett & Dee Eastman, Karen Lee-Thorp and Denise & Todd Wendorff.

Editorial and Art Direction: Rick Marschall
Production Coordinator: Nicole Davis
Edited: Vicki Newby
Cover and interior design: Tyler Mattson, NomadicMedia.net
Interior layouts, design management, production: Mark Rayburn, RayburnDesign.com
Proofreading: Vicki Newby and Linnea Lagerquist
Design Assistance: Katherine Spencer
Production Assistance: Roni Meek, Amy Aecovalle
Author photos: Brian Wiertzema and Art Zipple

Printed in the United States of America

05 06 07 08 09 // 10 9 8 7 6

ACKNOWLEDGMENTS

I'm thankful to the adult volunteers at Saddleback Church who are great small group leaders and to the students who are growing spiritually because they're connected to other believers. Good things are happening, and I'm so proud of you!

I'm thankful to the team at www.simplyyouthministry.com for working so hard to help create these types of resources that assist youth ministers and students throughout the world.

Gratitude for help on this project goes to Dennis Beckner, Kathleen Hamer, Erica Hamer, and especially Matt McGill who read every word of each book in the series and has made a big difference in my life and the books I write. What a joy to do life together with friends!

CONTENTS

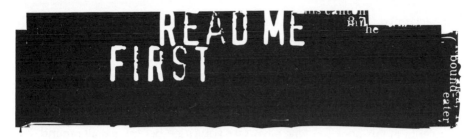

Welcome to a relational journey!

My prayer is that this book, a few friends, and a loving adult leader will take you on a journey that will revolutionize your life. The following six sessions were designed to help you grow as a Christian in the context of a caring, spiritual community. This community is a group of people committed to doing life together, at least for a season of your life. Spiritual community is formed when each small group member focuses on Jesus and the others in the group.

Creating spiritual community isn't easy. It requires trust, confidentiality, honesty, care, and commitment to meet regularly with your group. These are rare qualities in today's world. Any two or three people can meet together and call it a group, but it takes something special from you to create a community in which you can be known, be loved, be cared for, and feel safe enough to reveal thoughts, doubts, and struggles and still to be yourself. You may be tempted to show up at the small group session and sit, smile, and be nice, but never speak from your heart or say anything that would challenge another group member's thinking. This type of superficial participation prevents true spiritual community.

Most relationships never get beneath the relational surface. This LIFETOGETHER series is designed to push you to think, to talk, and to open your heart. You'll be challenged to expose some of your fears, hurts, and habits. As you do this, you'll find healing, experience spiritual growth, and build lasting, genuine friendships. Since God uses people to impact people you'll most likely become a richer, deeper, more vibrant person as you experience LIFETOGETHER with others. If you go through this book (and the 5 other books in this series) you will become a deeper and stronger follower of Jesus Christ. Get ready for something big to happen in your life!

WHAT YOU'LL FIND IN EACH SESSION

For each session, the group time contains five sections, one for each of the primary biblical purposes: fellowship, discipleship, ministry, evangelism, and worship. The five purposes can each stand alone, but when they're fused together, they make a greater impact on you and your world than the five of them might if approached separately. Think about it like this: If you play baseball or softball, you might be an outstanding hitter, but you also need to be able to catch, throw, run, and slide. You need more than one skill to make an impact for your team. In the same way, the five purposes individually are good, but when you put them all together, you're a balanced player who makes a huge impact.

The material in this book (and the other LIFETOGETHER books) is built around God's Word. You'll find a lot of blank spaces and journaling pages where you can write down your thoughts about God's work in your life as you explore and live out God's purposes.

Here's a closer look at what you'll find in these five sections:

FELLOWSHIP: CONNECTING Your Heart to Others'
[goal: to have students share about their lives and listen attentively to others]

These questions give you and the members of your small group a chance to share from your own lives, to get to know one another better, and to offer initial thoughts on the session theme. The picture for this section is a heart because you're opening up your heart so others can connect with you on a deeper level.

DISCIPLESHIP: GROWING to Be Like Jesus
[goal: to explore God's Word, learn biblical knowledge, and make personal applications]

This is the time to explore the Bible, gain biblical knowledge, and discuss how God's Word can make a difference in your life. The picture for this section is a brain because you're opening your mind to learn God's Word and ways.

You'll find lots of questions in this section; more than you can discuss during your group time. Your leader will choose the questions your group will discuss. You can respond to the other questions on your own during the week, which is a great way to get more Bible study. (See **At Home This Week** on page 29.)

MINISTRY: SERVING Others in Love
[goal: to recognize and take opportunities to serve others]

During each small group session, you'll have an opportunity to discuss how to meet needs by serving others. As you grow spiritually, you'll begin to recognize—and take—opportunities to serve others. As your heart expands, so will your opportunities to serve. Here, the picture is a foot because you're moving your feet to meet the needs of others.

EVANGELISM: SHARING Your Story and God's Story
[goal: to consider how the truths from this lesson might be applied to our relationships with unbelievers]

It's too easy for a small group to become a clique and only care about one another. That's not God's plan for us. He wants us to reach out to people with the good news. Each session will give you an opportunity to discuss your relationships with unbelievers and consider ways to reach out to them. The picture for this section is a mouth because you're opening your mouth to have spiritual conversations with unbelievers.

WORSHIP: SURRENDERING Your Life to Honor God
[goal: to focus on God's presence]

Each small group session ends with a time of prayer. You'll be challenged to slow down and turn your focus toward God's love, his goodness, and his presence in your life. You'll spend time talking to God, listening in silence, and giving your heart to him. Surrender is giving up what you want so God can give you what he wants. The picture for this section is a body, which represents you surrendering your entire life to God.

AT HOME THIS WEEK

At the end of each session, you'll find reminders of ways you can help yourself grow spiritually until your small group meets again. You're free to vary the options you choose from week to week. You'll find more information about each of these options near the end of the first session.

Daily Bible Readings

Page 108 contains a list of Bible passages to help you continue to take God's Word deeper in your life.

Memory Verses

On page 112 you'll find six Bible verses to memorize, one related to the topic of each session.

Journaling

Use **SCRIBBLE** pages, 117-125

You're offered several options to trigger your thoughts, including a question or two related to the topic of the session. Journaling is a great way to reflect on what you've been learning or to evaluate it.

Wrap It Up

Each session contains a lot of discussion questions, too many for one small group meeting. So you can think through your answers to the extra questions during the week.

LEARN A LITTLE MORE

You might want to learn a little more (hey, great title for a subsection!) about terms and phrases in the Bible passage. You'll find helpful information here.

FOR FURTHER STUDY

One of the best ways to understand Bible passages is by reading other verses on the same topic. You'll find suggestions here.

BEING IN A SMALL GROUP

You probably have enough casual or superficial friendships and don't need to waste your time cultivating more. To benefit the most from your small group time and to build great relationships, here are some ideas to help you:

Prepare to participate

Interaction is a key to a good small group. Talking too little will make it hard for others to get to know you. Everyone has something to contribute—yes, even you! But participating doesn't mean dominating, so be careful to not monopolize the conversation! Most groups typically have one conversation hog, and if you don't know who it is in your small group, then it might be you. Here's a tip: you don't have to answer every question and comment on every point. The bottom line is to find a balance between the two extremes.

Be consistent

Healthy relationships take time to grow. Quality time is great, but a great *quantity* of time is probably better. Plan to show up every week (or whenever your group plans to meet), even when you don't feel like it With only six sessions per book, if you miss just two meetings you'll have missed 33 percent of the small group times for this book. When you make a commitment to your small group a high priority, you're sure to build meaningful relationships.

Practice honesty and confidentiality

Strong relationships are only as solid as the trust they are built upon. Although it may be difficult, take a risk and be honest with your answers. God wants you to be known by others! Then respect the risks others are taking and offer them the same love, grace, and forgiveness God does. Make confidentiality a nonnegotiable value for your small group. Nothing kills community like gossip.

Come prepared

You can always arrive prepared by praying ahead of time. Ask God to give you the courage to be honest and the discipline to be respectful of others.

You aren't required to do any preparation in the workbook before you arrive (unless you're the leader—and then it's just a few minutes). But you may want to work through the **Growing** questions before your group time. Talk about this idea with your leader. If your group is going to do this, don't view the preparation as homework but as an opportunity to learn more about yourself and God to prepare yourself to go deeper.

Congratulations...

...on making a commitment to go through this material with your small group! Life change is within reach when people are united through the same commitment. Your participation in a small group can have a lasting and powerful impact on your life. Our prayer is that the questions and activities in this book help you grow closer to the other group members, and more importantly, to grow closer to God.

Doug Fields & Brett Eastman

Doug and Brett were part of the same small group for several years. Brett was the pastor of small groups at Saddleback Church where Doug is the pastor to students. Brett and a team of friends wrote Doing LifeTogether, a group study for adults. Everyone loved it so much that they asked Doug to revise it for students. So even though Brett and Doug both had a hand in this book, it's written as though Doug were sitting with you in your small group. For more on Doug and Brett see page 144.

FOR SMALL GROUP LEADERS

As the leader, prepare yourself by reading through the lesson and thinking about how you might lead it. The questions are a guide for you to help students grow spiritually. Think through which questions are best for your group. No curriculum author knows your students better than you. This small amount of preparation will help you manage the time you'll have together.

How to Go through Each Lesson

This book was written to be more like a guidebook than a workbook. In most workbooks, you're supposed to answer every question and fill in all the blanks. In this book, there are lots of questions and plenty of space.

Rule number one is that there are no rules about how you must go through the material. Every small group is unique and will figure out its own style and system. (The exception is when the lead youth worker establishes a guideline for all the groups to follow. In that case, respect your leader and conform your group to the leader's guidelines).

If you need a standard to get you started until you navigate your own way, this is how we used the material for a 60-minute session.

Intro (4 minutes)
Begin each session with one student reading the **Small Group Covenant** (see page 92). This becomes a constant reminder of why you're doing what you're doing. Then have another student read the opening paragraphs of the session you'll be discussing. Allow different students to take turns reading these two opening pieces.

Connecting (10 minutes)
This section can take 45 minutes if you're not careful to manage the time. You'll need to lead to keep this segment short. Consider giving students a specific amount of time and hold them to it. It's always better to leave students wanting more time for an activity than to leave them tired and bored.

Growing (25 minutes)
Read God's Word and work through the questions you think will be best for your group. This section will usually have more questions than you are able to discuss. Before the small group begins, take time to read through the questions to choose the best ones for your group. You may want to add questions of your own.

Serving and Sharing (10 minutes)
We typically choose one of these two sections to skip if pressed for time. If you decide to skip one or the other, group members can finish the section on their own during the week. Don't feel guilty about passing over a section. One of the strengths of this material is the built-in, intentional repetition. You'll have other opportunities to discuss that biblical purpose.

Surrendering (10 minutes)
We always want to end the lesson with a focus on God and a specific time of prayer. You'll be given several options, but you can always default to your group's comfort level to finish your time.

Closing Challenge (1 minute)
We encourage the students to pick one option from the **At Home This Week** section

that they'll do on their own. The more often students are able to take the initiative and develop the habit of spending time with God, the healthier they will be in their spiritual journey. We've found that students have plenty of unanswered questions that they want to go back and consider on their own.

Keep in Mind

- The main goal of this book isn't to have group members answer every question. The goal is **spiritual growth.**
- Make whatever adjustments you think are necessary.
- It's your small group, it's your time, and the questions will always be there. Use them, ignore them, or assign them to be answered during the week.
- Don't feel the pressure to have everyone answer every question.
- Questions are a great way to get students connecting to one another and God's Word.

Suggestions for Existing Small Groups

If your small group has been meeting for a while and you've already established comfortable relationships, you can jump right into the material. Make sure you take the following actions, even if you're a well-established group:

- Read through the **Small Group Covenant** on page 92 and make additions or adjustments.
- Read the **Prayer Request Guidelines** together (on page 128). You can maximize the group's time by following these guidelines.
- Consider whether you're going to assign the material to be completed (or at least thought through) before each meeting.
- Familiarize yourself with all the **At Home This Week** options that follow each lesson. They are detailed near the end of Session 1 (page 29) and summarized after the other five lessons.

Although handling business like this can seem cumbersome or unnecessary to an existing group, these foundational steps can save you from headaches later because you took the time to create an environment conducive to establishing deep relationships.

Suggestions for New Small Groups

If your group is meeting together for the first time, jumping right into the first lesson may not be your best option. You might want to have a meeting before you begin going through the book so you can get to know each other. To prepare for the first gathering, read and follow the **Suggestions for Existing Groups.**

When you get together with your group members, spend time getting to know one another by using ice-breaker questions. Several are listed here. Pick one or two that will work best for your group. Or you may have ice breakers of your own that you'd like to use. The goal is to break ground in order to plant the seeds of healthy relationships.

Ice Breakers

1 What's your name, school, grade, and favorite class in school? (Picking your least favorite class is too easy.)

2 Tell the group a brief (basic) history of your family. What's your family life like? How many brothers and sisters do you have? Which family members are you closest to?

3 What's one thing about yourself that you really like?

4 Everyone has little personality quirks—strange and unique habits that other people usually laugh about. What are yours?

5 Why did you choose to be a part of this small group?

6 What do you hope to get out of this small group? How do you expect it to help you?

7 In your opinion, what do you think it will take to make our small group work?

Great resources are available to help you!

Companion DVDs are available for the LifeTogether small group books. These DVDs contain teaching segments you can use to supplement each session by playing them before your small group discussion begins or just prior to the Growing to Be Like Jesus discussion. Some of my favorite youth ministry communicators in the world are included on these DVDs. (See page 140.)

In addition to the teaching segments on the DVDs, we've added small group leader tips that are unique to each session. Brett and I give you specific small group pointers and ideas that will help you lead each session. If you spend five to 10 minutes watching the leadership tips and then spend another 10 to 15 minutes reading through each session in advance, you'll be fully equipped to lead students through the material. The DVDs aren't required, but they're a great supplement to the small group material.

In addition, you can find free, helpful tips for leading small groups on our Web site, www.simplyyouthministry.com/lifetogether. These tips are general, so any small group leader may benefit from them. I encourage you to take advantage of these resources!

What STARTING TO GO WHERE GOD WANTS YOU TO BE is all about

Starting to Go Where God Wants You to Be begins with a call to love God and love others, followed by one session on each of the five biblical purposes: fellowship, discipleship, ministry, evangelism, and worship. It's like a table set with great appetizers. You get to taste them all.

I encourage small groups to begin with **Starting to Go Where God Wants You to Be.** Then study the rest of the books in any order—maybe by interest, maybe in an order that prepares you for events on the youth ministry calendar, such as **Sharing Your Story and God's Story** before an evangelism outreach in the fall or **Serving Others in Love** to prepare for the mission trip in the spring. With five other books to choose from, you're in control. There's no "correct" order for using the books.

You're ready to get started!

LIFE TOGETHER STUDENT EDITION

SHARING

YOUR STORY AND GOD'S STORY

DEVELOPING A HEART OF COMPASSION

Evangelism is a weird word and a scary thing to do for most Christians. Just about every Christian I've talked with feels uneasy about talking to others about God's plan through Jesus Christ. As you begin a book on evangelism, it would be normal if you had many fears, questions, and experiences rattling through your brains.

Some may fear that evangelism means learning Bible verses and knocking on doors to convert strangers. Others may have concerns about the difficult questions non-Christians will ask: *What's the deal with evolution? If God is loving, why do bad things happen to good people? Why don't marshmallows grow on trees?* Some in your group may have had previous negative experiences trying to share their faith and just don't want to do it again. I know exactly how you feel. I've been there too.

It's my prayer that as you discuss evangelism you'll learn it isn't about trying to convert strangers with memorized tactics. God is the one who changes lives—that's his job. Your privilege, as a Christian, is to develop friendships with others and through a series of stories gently guide them to the God who loves them more than you can imagine. Your "job" is to do what's possible while having faith that God will do the impossible—transform a life. You can do your part!

A healthy discussion of evangelism begins with the "why question." Why evangelism? The Bible provides answers, and as we pursue them we're going to start with developing a biblical understanding of God's awesome love for people. God's love is so different from human love that it can change a life. Human love can influence a life, but God's love can transform a heart, which will redirect a life. And the wild thing about God's transforming love is that he can do it with any life, no matter how bad it might be. Even the worst are within reach of God's love. You might consider someone out of God's reach. God doesn't, and he might choose you to reach them. You never know! Let the journey begin.

FELLOWSHIP: CONNECTING Your Heart to Others'

[goal: to have students share about their lives and listen attentively to others]

Few people come to Christ without any human assistance. Most people can point back to at least one person who shined some light on Christ, Christianity, or a lifestyle that was an influential witness to living God's way.

1 Who is the person who most influenced your commitment to follow Jesus? How did this person impact your life? (Remember to keep your response brief so everyone will have a chance to share.)

2 Do you think many of your non—Christian friends are open to having spiritual conversations? Explain why or why not. Do you find it difficult to talk about God with others? Why do you think that is?

If there are people in your small group who are new to the Christian faith, they should be encouraged to reread page 21 to make sure they understand our working definition of evangelism so they'll be prepared to engage in the upcoming discussions.

If you haven't discussed the **Small Group Covenant** on page 92, take time to read it together and discuss it now. Make commitments to one another that your group time will reflect those values. You may want to have one person read the covenant to the group before you begin each lesson as a reminder.

Use the **Small Group Roster** (page 94) to record the names and contact information of the small group members.

DISCIPLESHIP: GROWING to Be Like Jesus

[goal: to explore God's Word, learn biblical knowledge, and make personal applications]

Sharing the good news about salvation through faith in Jesus—evangelism—begins with a very distinct attitude or condition of one's heart. It's called compassion. Compassion is the attitude that recognizes the true spiritual condition and needs of people. We are lost and without hope. The following passage reveals the compassion of our model, Jesus.

> ³⁵Jesus went through all the towns and villages, teaching in their synagogues, preaching the good news of the kingdom and healing every disease and sickness. ³⁶When he saw the crowds, he had compassion on them, because they were harassed and helpless, like sheep without a shepherd. ³⁷Then he said to his disciples, "The harvest is plentiful but the workers are few. ³⁸Ask the Lord of the harvest, therefore, to send out workers into his harvest field."
>
> —Matthew 9:35-38

Terms that look like this are described in Learn a Little More near the end of the session.

What do you think made a bigger impact on the crowds, Jesus' teaching or his miracles? Explain why you think so.

4

5

What's the difference between feeling sorry for someone and feeling compassion for him?

6

Since the crowds had the teaching and wisdom of Jesus, how could they be "harassed and helpless" and "without a shepherd?" Wasn't Jesus their shepherd?

Would you consider yourself to be a compassionate person? Why do you think that?

7

8

Is it possible to be too compassionate? Explain.

What are some common obstacles people must overcome to be more compassionate?

9

What would a compassionate person look like in your everyday life (at home, at school, in sports, on the job...)?

Why does Jesus say that the harvest is plentiful but the workers are few? Does this mean some people won't be harvested because there are too few workers? What are the implications of your answer to this question?

What's the ultimate destiny for those without faith in Jesus? When you think about specific people you know, how do you feel?

If you fail to share the gospel with someone, does this mean it's your fault if he or she never makes a commitment of faith in Jesus? Explain your answer.

MINISTRY: SERVING Others in Love

[goal: to recognize and take opportunities to serve others]

As you develop a heart for those living without Christ, it helps to understand the needs of others.

If God's efforts to bring people into his kingdom are not limited by our human efforts, why should we concern ourselves with being evangelistic?

What are the basic needs of the people who live within your community? What about the needs of those within your school community? What are the needs of unbelievers?

15

In what practical ways can you begin to meet those needs?

16

EVANGELISM: SHARING Your Story and God's Story

[goal: to consider how the truths from this lesson might be applied to relationships with unbelievers]

Having compassion for others isn't something that comes naturally to most of us. When God lives within your heart, you'll begin to see others in the way God sees them. That's one of the goals of being a follower of Jesus—to be more like him.

In an attempt to develop a heart for non-Christians, it's good to begin thinking of those you know who don't have a relationship with God. When they're on your mind, they'll begin to make their way into your heart.

"NO WAY!" Make two lists. In the first list write names of public figures—people you don't know personally (actors, athletes, teachers, politicians...)—about whom you assume by their lifestyle that they probably don't have a relationship with God.

In the second list write names of people you know personally who are the type of people who cause you to think, "No way is that person a Christian. I don't think this person would want anything to do with Jesus." (Think through different areas of your life: school, family, neighborhood, work, sports teams...)

17

```
PUBLIC FIGURES




```

```
PERSONAL ACQUAINTANCES
```

(You may want to use initials or code names if your book might be read by others.)

What are you currently doing to develop friendships with those people?

18

At the beginning of small groups such as this one, you should decide whether your group is open to inviting friends to join. If your group is open, list who you would like to invite and make plans for talking with them. Your small group leader or your leadership team may have already determined the group is closed at this time. If so, a good group respects and follows that decision. You may be able to invite friends to join you in the next LIFETOGETHER book.

Read How to Keep Your Small Group from Becoming a Clique (page 96) when you're at home.

Pray for the people in your second list above.

19

You'll find three prayer resources in the back of the book. By reading and discussing them, you'll find your group prayer time more rewarding.

- **Praying in Your Small Group** (page 126). Read this on your own before the next session.
- **Prayer Request Guidelines** (page 128). Read and discuss these guidelines as a group.
- **Prayer Options** (page 130). Refer to this list for ideas to give your prayer time variety.

Before your group breaks, read **At Home This Week** together. (If everyone in the group has already done this in another LifeTogether book, you can skip the introduction if you'd like.)

WORSHIP: SURRENDERING Your Life to Honor God

[goal: to focus on God's presence]

Compassion for others seems to flow from those who have a growing and intimate relationship with Jesus...the True Shepherd. Typically you'll discover that your evangelistic efforts will increase as your faith grows stronger. When you're most connected to Jesus is when you'll be most sensitive to seeing others connect to God.

Have each person share one specific way the others in the group can pray for them. This is a time to write down prayer requests on the **Prayer Request Log** (page 132). Pray for one another that this small group time will help you grow in your relationship with God and that you'll learn more about what it means to care for the lost sheep in your world.

AT HOME THIS WEEK

Each week, you'll have at least four options to help you grow and learn on your own—which means you'll have more to contribute when you return to the group.

Daily Bible Readings

On page 108 you'll find **Daily Bible Readings,** a chart of Bible passages that correspond with the lessons—five for each week. If you choose this option, read one passage each day. Highlight it in your Bible, reflect on it, journal about it, or repeat it out loud as a prayer. You're free to interact with the Bible verses any way you want, just be sure to read God's love letter—the Bible. You'll find helpful tips in **How to Study the Bible** (page 109).

Memory Verses

Memorizing Bible verses is an important habit to develop as you learn to grow spiritually on your own. **Memory Verses** (page 112) lists six verses—one per week—for you to memorize if you want to plant God's Word in your heart. Memorizing verses (and making them stick for more than a few minutes) isn't easy, but the benefits are undeniable. You'll have God's Word with you wherever you go.

Journaling

Use **SCRIBBLE** pages, 117-125

You'll find blank pages for journaling beginning on page 117. At the end of each session, you'll find several options and a question or two to get your thoughts going—but you aren't limited to the ideas in this book. Use these pages to reflect, to write a letter to God, to note what you're learning, to compose a prayer, to ask a question, to draw a picture of your praise, to record your thoughts. For more suggestions about journaling, turn to **Journaling: Snapshots of Your Heart** (page 114).

If you'd like to choose journaling this week, respond to this question: *What are your fears when you think about evangelism?*

Wrap It Up

Write out your answers to session questions your group didn't have time to discuss.

This week share with the others in your group which option seems most appealing to try during the coming week. The variety of preferences is another reminder of how different the people in your group are.

During other weeks, take time to share with the group what you did **At Home This Week.**

LEARN A LITTLE MORE

Synagogues

"During [the time of Jesus] the term 'synagogue' referred both to a group of people and a building or institution. The meeting place and prayer hall of the Jewish people."

> **The Anchor Bible Dictionary**, vol. 6, by D. N. Freedman (Doubleday, 1996).

Compassion

To be sympathetic to the distress of others with a desire to alleviate it. True compassion moves us to action. See James 5:11 and Psalm 103:13.

Sheep without a shepherd

Sheep are not intelligent animals. They have few natural defense mechanisms, which means they're low on the food chain. Without a shepherd to care for them, they are at the mercy of predators such as wolves, lions, and bears. This is an accurate picture of us without Christ. We are at the mercy of predators like the world, our desires, and Satan.

Harvest

Jesus uses the picture of a harvest to describe the gathering of people into the kingdom of God. When a crop isn't harvested at the proper time, the fruit falls to the ground and rots and becomes useless. The crops are people ready to believe in Jesus. Jesus has called all believers to work the field in order to harvest people for the kingdom. God is not dependent on our efforts, but he still calls us to work the field, not to stand on the sidelines.

FOR FURTHER STUDY

Luke 13:34; 23:28-43

NOTES

NOTES

BEHIND THE MASK

I remember a cheer from my high school years. I listened to it a lot because I had plenty of time to focus on everything happening in the stands from my position on the bench. As if it were yesterday, I can hear the cheer:

> What you see is what you get,
> and you ain't seen nothing yet!
> Go Spartans!

I knew it wasn't a true statement then, and it's still not true today.

For most people, what you see of them isn't really who they are. Typically what you see is a mask, a façade, a disguise. Your friends won't scream out, "I'm insecure and feel unloved." Instead they might act cocky or arrogant to hide their true feelings. That's safer. No one wants to be made fun of, so they answer tough questions from behind a mask: "Nothing. I don't know." *Nothing* is never the true answer. There's always something going on inside. There's more to people than what the human eye can see. When you see someone who's acting out, chances are good that he or she is hurting inside. People who hurt others are usually deeply hurt themselves and don't know how to live their lives without hurting others.

Jesus understands that people have more going on than one can see from the outside. Jesus was a master at getting behind the masks. He wasn't afraid of the tax collector whom everyone hated. Jesus recognized the loneliness he was experiencing because of his job. Jesus knew the woman at the well had a deeper thirst than water could satisfy.

As God prepares your heart to be evangelistic and you learn the importance of friendships, listening, sharing your story, and sharing God's story, you'll benefit from getting a grasp of this truth: what you see isn't all you get. Actually you're not seeing anything until you get behind a person's mask. Try to lift the masks in your conversations today to see if a little honesty brings some big changes to your small group.

FELLOWSHIP: CONNECTING Your Heart to Others'

Your friends have all kinds of needs in their lives—to belong, to be known, to be loved, to be appreciated, to be valued. When needs aren't met, most people won't come out and say, "Do you love me?" Instead, they draw attention to themselves so that when they get attention they feel loved. Attention equals love for many people. (Be sure everyone in your small group understands how this substitution process works.)

Which of the following masks do you most relate to?
- My anger is often a disguise for my loneliness.
- My arrogance is often a disguise for feeling insecure and my need to be liked.
- My perfectionism is often a disguise for my need to control my surroundings.
- My moodiness is my way to get attention.
- Other _____

Do you find it difficult to go deep relationally with your non–Christian friends? If so, why is it difficult to lift the masks? If not, what's your secret?

Without saying the person's name, think about a person you don't get along with, someone who tends to bother you every time you're around him or her. What might be that person's deepest needs?
- If you have no clue about the person's real needs, what could you do to find out? Think creatively. Come up with something besides, "I could talk to him."

DISCIPLESHIP: GROWING to Be Like Jesus

Jesus was a master at seeing past people's defenses and into their hearts. In this passage you'll see how he zeroed in on the real needs of a Samaritan woman.

2

⁴Now [Jesus] had to go through Samaria. ⁵So he came to a town in Samaria called Sychar, near the plot of ground Jacob had given to his son Joseph. ⁶Jacob's well was there, and Jesus, tired as he was from the journey, sat down by the well. It was about the sixth hour.

⁷When a Samaritan woman came to draw water, Jesus said to her, "Will you give me a drink?" ⁸(His disciples had gone into the town to buy food.)

⁹The Samaritan woman said to him, "You are a Jew and I am a Samaritan woman. How can you ask me for a drink?" (For Jews do not associate with Samaritans.)

¹⁰Jesus answered her, "If you knew the gift of God and who it is that asks you for a drink, you would have asked him and he would have given you living water."

¹¹"Sir," the woman said, "you have nothing to draw with and the well is deep. Where can you get this living water? ¹²Are you greater than our father Jacob, who gave us the well and drank from it himself, as did also his sons and his flocks and herds?"

¹³Jesus answered, "Everyone who drinks this water will be thirsty again, ¹⁴but whoever drinks the water I give him will never thirst. Indeed, the water I give him will become in him a spring of water welling up to eternal life."

¹⁵The woman said to him, "Sir, give me this water so that I won't get thirsty and have to keep coming here to draw water."

¹⁶He told her, "Go, call your husband and come back."

¹⁷"I have no husband," she replied.

Jesus said to her, "You are right when you say you have no husband. ¹⁸The fact is, you have had five husbands, and the man you now have is not your husband. What you have just said is quite true."

¹⁹"Sir," the woman said, "I can see that you are a prophet. ²⁰Our fathers worshiped on this mountain, but you Jews claim that the place where we must worship is in Jerusalem."

²¹Jesus declared, "Believe me, woman, a time is coming when you will worship the Father neither on this mountain nor in Jerusalem. ²²You Samaritans worship what you do not know; we worship what we do know, for salvation is from the Jews. ²³Yet a time is coming and has now come when the true worshipers will worship the Father in spirit and truth, for they are the kind of worshipers the Father seeks. ²⁴God is spirit, and his worshipers must worship in spirit and in truth."

²⁵The woman said, "I know that Messiah" (called Christ) "is coming. When he comes, he will explain everything to us."

²⁶Then Jesus declared, "I who speak to you am he."

²⁷Just then his disciples returned and were surprised to find him talking with a woman. But no one asked, "What do you want?" or

"Why are you talking with her?"
28Then, leaving her water jar, the woman went back to the town and said to the people, 29"Come, see a man who told me everything I ever did. Could this be the Christ?"

—John 4:4-29

What do you find most interesting about this dialogue?

4

Why does it matter that the woman was a Samaritan? What clues are in the text that being a Samaritan is significant?

5

What is John's reason for telling us the time of this event in verse 6?

6

Why might Jesus have asked for a drink?

7

What's living water? What does it do?

8

Why did Jesus ask the Samaritan woman about her husband and then bring up her past marriages? How could Jesus do this and keep the woman interested in having a conversation with him?

9

According to verse 20, what's one difference between the Samaritans and the Jews?

10

11

How does Jesus respond to the woman's attempt to change the subject in verse 20? Why does he respond this way?

What do you imagine this woman's needs were? Be as specific as you can. Examine her dialogue to discover what she felt like she needed, and look at Jesus' responses to see what she really needed.

12

13

At the end of this conversation, Jesus claims to be the Messiah (Christ). Why didn't he just start out the conversation by explaining this to the woman?

How might this passage impact the way you approach evangelism? Can you identify any specific strategies that Jesus used with this woman?

14

MINISTRY: SERVING Others in Love

Some of the action steps that will help you be more evangelistic are basic friendship skills that you can practice. This week you can serve others and practice your skills by considering ways to meet needs of others.

15 Turn to **Listening Like Jesus** (page 90) and read it with a partner and discuss how you might be able to apply some of Jesus' actions to your life situation this week.

16 Go back to the list of names you wrote during the last session (pages 26 and 27) to see if you can identify what their real needs might be. When you made the list you were thinking, "No way! She'll never give her life to God." Without turning this action into a gossip fest, try to identify what needs they might be hiding behind their masks.

17 As a group, share some of the needs (without using the names) and discuss ways that those needs might be addressed when talking about Jesus.

18 This week, approach one person (preferably from your list on page 27) to see if you can do something to meet a practical need and enhance your friendship. It might be helping with homework, giving a ride, carrying packages or books—anything that meets a practical need.

When you begin meeting needs in practical ways you'll get closer to the deeper emotional, relational, and spiritual needs that your friends have

EVANGELISM: SHARING Your Story and God's Story

As a Christian, you know that Jesus is the answer to the true needs of people. So when you know a person's true needs (what's behind the mask), you'll have greater sensitivity when you two talk about how Jesus can meet the needs.

Here are examples:

I will pray daily for _____ [an unchurched relative or friend].

I will take time to show love to _____ in a practical way.

I will practice my listening and observation skills in an attempt to better understand the needs of others.

I will begin to share my story about my need for Jesus with one unchurched friend.

I will write out the story of what God has done in my life.

I will pray each day [or week] for the people on pages 26 and 27.

Write your goal here:

As you walk through your campus or your neighborhood look closely at those who act out. Instead of quickly moving past them and muttering to yourself, "What a jerk," stop and consider what might be broken on their inside world that motivates them to act that way. This week, become conscious of those who are acting out. Ask God to help you better understand what's behind the masks of others. Be patient. Be ready to share some of your new insight the next time your group meets.

Write down one evangelistic goal you think God might like you to focus on during the next 30 days. What might you do to reach that goal?

WORSHIP: SURRENDERING Your Life to Honor God

Pair up with someone in your small group and discuss these two questions:

What's hot? (In what ways are you doing well spiritually?)

What's not? (In which areas do you need the most growth?)

For the rest of the weeks your group is working through this book, let this person be your spiritual partner. Whenever your group breaks into pairs again, get together with your spiritual partner.

It's a normal part of group life to have a closer connection with some people than with others. If you find this to be the case and you'd like to spend more time throughout the week talking about life and challenging one another spiritually, consider using the **Accountability Questions** on page 98.

Stay with your spiritual partner for prayer. Take a few minutes to share prayer requests that haven't come up in your discussion. Then pray for each other, especially for the strength to follow through on your evangel- istic goals.

Take some time this week to answer the questions on the **Spiritual Health Assessment** (pages 99-107). The goal is to evaluate your spiritual journey honestly, not to get a high score. If you don't have time to write answers for all the questions, make sure you at least circle the numbers on the scale that best apply to you. (It should only take a few minutes.) You may have the opportunity to share your results during your next session.

AT HOME THIS WEEK

Daily Bible Readings
Check out the Scriptures on page 108.

Memory Verses
Try memorizing a verse from page 112.

Journaling

Use **SCRIBBLE** pages, 117-125

- 🔖 Write whatever is on your mind.
- 🔖 Read your journal entry from last week and write a reflection on it.
- 🔖 Respond to this question: *What's behind the masks I wear that I'm afraid to let people know about?*

Wrap It Up

Write out your answers to session questions your group didn't have time to discuss.

LEARN A LITTLE MORE

Just as we do today, people in Jesus' time were quick to notice ethnic differences and divide the world into *us* and *them* (such as Jews and Samaritans). They saw ethnic differences as a reason to look down on others. Jesus ignored those barriers in a way that was unheard of in his day. He simply saw people with needs.

Samaria...Samaritan woman

Verse 9 gives us the necessary background information we need to understand the heart of what was happening between Jesus and this woman: "For Jews do not associate with Samaritans." The Jews considered Samaritans "half breeds." Their ancestors were Jews who had married non-Jews. A Jewish person during the time of Jesus would go to great lengths to avoid any contact with a Samaritan. This Scripture says, "Now [Jesus] had to go through Samaria." The original readers would have found this ironic because he could have walked around Samaria as *every other* Jewish teacher would have done.

In addition to crossing this racial barrier, Jesus also broke down others. It wasn't accepted for a rabbi (spiritual teacher) to have extended conversations with women, as Jewish culture heavily segregated men and women. The woman at the well was probably a social outcast since she went to the well during the hottest part of the day. Since she led an immoral life, most people, especially religious people, would have avoided her.

Jesus let nothing stop him from sharing the truth with this woman: differences in race, gender, or social status were hurdles that he overcame.

Jacob...Joseph

Jacob and Joseph were important men in the history of the Jews and Samaritans. They were founding fathers and therefore worthy of respect. Verses 5 and 6 (about Jacob's well) set up the scene to give perspective for verse 12 ("Are you greater than Jacob?"). While Jacob was great and could provide a physical well of fresh water, Jesus was greater and was the source of eternal life.

Sixth hour
About noon.

Our fathers worshiped on this mountain
Cut off from Jewish society, the Samaritans developed their own religious traditions. As you might expect, this became another reason for Jewish people to disassociate themselves from the Samaritans. They had also corrupted the Jewish religion.

Let's go deep: Jesus confronted the woman with her immoral life, and while he did this in an inoffensive way, the woman was definitely uncomfortable. What is the normal response in a conversation when things get uncomfortable? Change the subject—which she does. It's more important to understand that the woman is changing the subject than to know the background information about Samaritan religious practices.

God is spirit, and his worshipers must worship in spirit and in truth
If you were to ask 50 different Christians from 50 different churches what it means to worship God, you'd probably get 50 different responses. People are different and therefore worship God in a variety of styles. There's nothing wrong with that.

But when the woman changes the subject, Jesus refuses to get caught up in a debate about external forms or styles of worship. He jumps right to the heart of the matter: Worship isn't about a particular place or ritual. It's about believing God is who he says he is and believing what he has done.

When we're talking with non-Christians, it's best to stick to the ideas that are most important. Explaining the different theologies about communion or a precise chronology of the end times probably aren't the truths a non-Christian needs to be wrestling with. Issues like those are "changing the subject."

FOR FURTHER STUDY

Luke 19:1-10
Mark 10:17-22

NOTES

NOTES

BUILDING FRIENDSHIPS

At church, people expect me to talk about Jesus because they know I'm a pastor. In my full-time Christian work environment, my evangelistic efforts are minimal because most people I'm with all day are already followers of Christ. To be evangelistic I must get involved and build friendships within my community. That's one of the reasons I coach my kids' sports teams. As a Little League or soccer coach no one expects me to talk about Jesus. Parents are anticipating that I'll teach their children the fundamentals of the sport and treat them kindly.

Typically by the end of each season, most of the players and parents have become friends and have heard me relate my story of faith to their current story as well as God's story. I don't say, "I'm going to teach you about baseball and Jesus. Grab your gloves, and let's pray." I do my job and teach the sport. After every practice and game, I talk to parents, I encourage their kids, I inquire about their lives, I listen to their problems, I try to get behind the masks by listening carefully for their real needs. Basically I'm taking the time and opportunities to make friends. Usually after several weeks, the occasion for a discussion about Jesus is natural, and I have many opportunities for spiritual conversations. These friendships have taught me that non-Christians aren't afraid of Jesus, they're afraid of church and Christians. After we've developed friendships and when they learn that I care about them, I'm able to share the reasons I'm a Christian and how I badly needed God's overwhelming love in my life.

Friendships and spending time hanging together will make the difference in creating opportunities for you to talk about Jesus. If you can take steps to build friendships, you *will* have opportunities for spiritual conversations. That's what this small group lesson is all about—identifying friendship qualities and how friends tell friends their stories.

FELLOWSHIP: CONNECTING Your Heart to Others'

Evangelism doesn't have to be an extra spiritual activity. Instead you can share your story when it's natural and appropriate in the midst of your normal, everyday life.

Rate yourself on the following scale:

1   2   3   4   5   6   7   8   9   10

all my friends are Christians   all my friends are unbelievers

What's your typical attitude about non–Christians?

During a regular week, when and where do you interact with non–Christians?

Think of one person in your life who doesn't believe in Christ. Imagine how you might begin a spiritual conversation with that person. What thoughts or feelings go through your mind when you imagine that?

DISCIPLESHIP: GROWING to Be Like Jesus

As a Christian, you have been gifted with a new eternal life because of your faith in Jesus Christ. You can't earn this gift, so you don't have to live according to the wishes of others in order to please God. Your salvation isn't based on what other people think about you.

While your salvation is in Christ, your ability to influence others *is* directly related to what they think about you. You can't walk up to athletes at your school, make fun of their sport, their shorts, and their lousy record, and then hope to share the gospel.

The apostle Paul understood what it took to influence others for Jesus.

46   SHARING your story and God's story

¹⁹Even though I am free of the demands and expectations of everyone, I have voluntarily become a servant to any and all in order to reach a wide range of people: ²⁰religious, nonreligious, ²¹meticulous moralists, loose-living immoralists, the defeated, the demoralized—whoever. I didn't take on their way of life. I kept my bearings in Christ—but I entered their world and tried to experience things from their point of view. ²²I've become just about every sort of servant there is in my attempts to lead those I meet into a God-saved life. ²³I did all this because of the Message. I didn't just want to talk about it; I wanted to be in on it!

—1 Corinthians 9:19-23 THE MESSAGE

5 In this passage, it's clear that becoming a servant includes building relationships with others. Why does Paul talk about freedom? What does freedom have to do with befriending others?

6 What does it mean to enter their world but not take on their way of life?

📖 Give an example of a time when you were able to enter someone else's life and not take on her way of life.

📖 Give an example of a time when you entered into someone else's life but he influenced you negatively more than you influenced him for Jesus.

7 Paul entered into the world of others for the Message (for the sake of the gospel). Why might Christians criticize this approach today?

8 What's an illustration of our freedom in Christ going too far?

9 What type of people do you find it easy to connect with? What type of people do you find it difficult to connect with?

10 What are the implications from this passage for your friendships? How are you personally challenged?

11 Read the NIV translation of verse 22: "To the weak I became weak, to win the weak. I have become all things to all men so that by all possible means I might save some." Why isn't a person like this a fake, a relational chameleon who changes depending on who she's with at the moment?

12 How can we be close friends with non-Christians without letting them influence us negatively?

What do you think the apostle Paul would say to Christians who would like to go the easy route and only spend time with fellow Christians who share their values and interests?

13

What are your honest feelings about spending more time and developing friendships with unbelievers?

14

3

MINISTRY: SERVING Others in Love

Friendships begin in a variety of ways and often for unusual reasons. Regardless of how they start, friendships must possess certain qualities to maintain the relationship.

List some qualities of a healthy friendship.

15

Next to each quality, write down the name of a person you know who captures this quality in his or her life.

16

Here is your ministry opportunity to serve another in love: choose one person from your list and write this person a letter or send him an e-mail this week. Encourage your friend about a positive quality you see in him and what you appreciate about your friendship. Encouragement is one of the qualities that develop good friendships. You'll minister to your friend by your encouraging e-mail or letter.

 # EVANGELISM: SHARING Your Story and God's Story

Telling others about God's love is something that comes naturally to a few, but most of us need to learn different ways to share about God with others. The best way to learn how to have evangelistic conversations is to practice them. This may feel awkward, but most skills require practice.

Imagine a friend says, "I'm kind of interested in learning more about God and the Bible. I've been thinking about it a lot lately. Why are you a Christian?" Before you give your answer, take 60 seconds to write down some key words, ideas, or verses that you might share with this person.

Pair up with your spiritual partner and share what you would say to your inquiring friend. Afterward give each other feedback about how you responded. (Don't be too hard on each other since you're not pros at turning normal conversation into spiritual conversations yet.)

SHARING your story and God's story

WORSHIP: SURRENDERING Your Life to Honor God

Share prayer requests with one another. Write them down on the **Prayer Request Log** (page 132).

Spend time in prayer thanking God for the friendships you have, for the courage to begin new ones, and for the wisdom to know how to be a good listener and a caring person.

AT HOME THIS WEEK

Daily Bible Readings
Check out the Scriptures on page 108.

Memory Verses
Try memorizing a verse from page 112.

Journaling
Use **SCRIBBLE** pages, 117-125
- Write whatever is on your mind.
- Read your journal entry from last week and write a reflection on it.
- Respond to these questions: *What can I do to be a better friend? How can I become a better listener to my friends?*

Wrap It Up
Write out your answers to the session questions your group didn't have time to discuss.

LEARN A LITTLE MORE

I am free of the demands and expectations of everyone

Paul wanted to be clear that salvation isn't dependent on how we please others. We are saved by the grace of God through faith in the death and resurrection of Jesus. Living a life that influences others for the gospel is important. Every Christian should work toward this, but our status in God's family is not determined by it.

I have voluntarily become a servant to any and all...I entered their world and experienced things from their point of view

Consider Paul's life: he worked hard to relate well to just about everyone he met. Can you imagine the patience he must have shown others? To live at peace with such a wide range of people (meticulous moralists to loose-living immoralists), Paul wasn't easily offended because he refused to judge them.

If you are a mature believer, think deeply about the things that bother you about non-Christians. If you can let go of your "right" to be annoyed, you're likely to find more opportunities to share about Jesus. If you find that you spend most of your day disgusted by non-Christians, ask God to change your heart so you can influence theirs.

I didn't take their way of life. I kept my bearings in Christ

In our pursuit to relate to unbelievers, it's important to know just how far we should go. Paul clearly answers this question: Do whatever it takes to influence others for Christ (but we aren't motivated by a desire to earn our salvation) without going so far that we step off the solid foundation of Christ.

Maybe you have a friend who is using a street drug. You want to strive to be around that person without judging him but not partake in his activities. The excuse, "But mom, I was just smoking pot so I could reach my friend with the gospel," won't work.

FOR FURTHER STUDY

Philippians 1:27-30; 2:14-16
1 Thessalonians 2:5-12

NOTES

If you are watching the LifeTogether DVD, you may use this page to take notes.

NOTES

A friend invited me to his church when I was in ninth grade by explaining, "It'll be great! There are cute girls, food, and there's going to be a comedian." That invitation didn't require much thought on my part. I was there! Girls, food, and laughter. As a teenager that was my kind of church. That night my life was changed, but not the way I expected. I expected a girlfriend; instead I returned with a changed life.

After the comedian's routine, he shared his personal story of God invading, impacting, and influencing his life. Everything he said made me think about my life, my story, and how I really wanted what I heard about his life. I was captivated by his story, and I longed for the joy I could hear in his voice. As he was telling his story, he mixed in God's story—God's desire for a relationship with me. I had never heard it like that before. He wasn't preachy; he was conversational.

Three stories were woven together to open my eyes to God's ways and softened my heart to change: the comedian's story, God's story, my reflection on my own story. All three stories came colliding into my life and the lights went on. I got it! All the seeds that my friends planted through friendship and concern for me bore fruit that night as I was drawn to surrender my life to God (as much as I knew how at the time). There was life-changing power in those stories.

So far, throughout this book, we've looked at (1) developing compassion for those who are lost, (2) identifying the needs of people beneath their masks, and (3) creating friendships as a foundation for evangelism. In this session, you'll be talking about sharing your own story (or testimony) in the midst of a spiritual conversation. Effective evangelism can happen when God's story of salvation is made personal through your story of what he did in your life and why you needed him.

Everyone has a story to share, and because it's all about God working in your life, it's a *great story!* Your friends have their own ideas about God, and they have no reason to assume your ideas are any better informed than theirs. But because of your friendship, they're likely to be interested in knowing more about your story.

I want to encourage you to share your story as fearlessly and honestly as you can, not from a position of moral or spiritual superiority but as someone just like them—in need of a Savior. In doing this, it's possible that before long your friend will see they need a Savior too. Your story meets their story.

This is the point where the discussion of evangelism can begin to get a little scary. Make sure you encourage one another through this learning process. That's one of the benefits of being in a small group. You don't have to do all this alone.

FELLOWSHIP: CONNECTING Your Heart to Others'

What part of your story (how you came to have a personal relationship with Jesus) would make an interesting connection with a non-Christian?

> Your story may be dramatic, but it doesn't have to be. God can use your story no matter what. A clean, moral life shows the power of God for living, which draws some people. A dramatic turnaround displays the power of God to transform, which draws others.

DISCIPLESHIP: GROWING to Be Like Jesus

The thought of talking to a non-Christian about God makes most of us—me included—shake with fear. We begin to mumble incoherently and wish desperately for a safe place. Okay, maybe it's not that bad, but let's be honest: Evangelism is tough for 99 percent of Christians. It can seem impossible!

We can take the stress out of evangelism when we understand what God expects of us. He doesn't ask us to do something that's too difficult for us. Paul was the master of evangelism, so let's learn from him. It's not easy, but it's not impossible.

> ²Devote yourselves to prayer, being watchful and thankful. ³And pray for us, too, that God may open a door for our message, so that we may proclaim the mystery of Christ, for which I am in chains. ⁴Pray that I may proclaim it clearly, as I should. ⁵Be wise in the way you act toward outsiders; make the most of every opportunity. ⁶Let your conversation be always full of grace, seasoned with salt, so that you may know how to answer everyone.
> —Colossians 4:2-6

What seems to be the connection between prayer and sharing Paul's story?

Paul describes a way to pray: be watchful and thankful. What do these terms mean? What are we supposed to watch for? What should we be thankful about?

When it comes to your prayer life, what do you struggle with the most?
◇ I don't pray long enough.
◇ I don't know what to pray for.
◇ I don't pray consistently.
◇ I usually only pray for myself, not for other Christians.
◇ I don't pray for opportunities to share my faith.
◇ Other _____

Paul, one of the greatest evangelists who ever lived, asked others to pray for him so he might share the gospel clearly. Even though he was an expert, he still felt like he needed God's supernatural help.

What is the message of the gospel? If an unbeliever were in your small group today, how might you explain it?
▣ Where are the gaps in your knowledge? What seems unclear to you?

Have you recently missed (or avoided) an opportunity to have a spiritual conversation with a non–Christian? What happened?

If you haven't had any opportunities recently to have a spiritual conversation with an unbeliever, do you think this is because God isn't giving them to you or you're not seeing them? Explain your answer.

7

What does it mean to fill our conversations with grace? Why does Paul compare this with salt?

8

Our words carry so much power. We've all said things we regret. Are you the kind of person who thinks about what you say before you speak? Do you need to reflect more about your words before you say them?

9

Knowing "how to answer everyone" (verse 6) is the part that scares many Christians. Does this mean knowing the answer to every question? If not, what does it mean?

10

If a non-Christian asked you a question about your faith and you didn't know the answer, what would be a good way to handle the situation? Brainstorm some ideas.

MINISTRY: SERVING Others in Love

Serving non-Christians is the best way to open the doors to conver-

...sations about your story and God's story. Let's consider how our service can be evangelistic. Colossians 4:5 reads, "Be wise in the way that you act towards outsiders." What have you seen Christians do that wasn't wise—actions that hinder their chances of effectively sharing the gospel?

Go personal (even though it may be difficult): Is there anything you're doing to treat unbelievers in ways that might compromise your story? How might an attitude of servanthood impact the outcome?

EVANGELISM: SHARING Your Story and God's Story

Share some of the main points of your personal story. You may need to break into groups of three or four to give everyone a chance to share.

If you need some questions to trigger your thinking, consider these:
- What was my life like before I met Jesus?
- Why did I need Jesus?
- How did I realize my need for Jesus?
- How did I commit my life to Jesus?
- What difference has my relationship with Jesus made in my life?
- Who is someone I could share my story with this week?

After each person shares his or her story, give the person encouraging feed-back. Do your best to be specific in your comments. Help each other see parts where honesty enhances the story. Being real (honest) about one's life and journey is so much more attractive than a fake, canned, story.

This is not an opportunity to coach people toward better stories. It's simply your chance to be encouraging about the elements that impacted you.

Your story may create questions that you don't know how to answer, so be sure to read **When You Don't Have the Right Answers** (page 91) and discuss the questions with your group (or write answers on your own later). Even though it will help you with a strategy for difficult questions, you should also learn how to find out the answers so you can get back to your friend.

 # WORSHIP: SURRENDERING Your Life to Honor God

Spend your closing moments together and pray as a group. Each person can choose one of the ideas from the list below or you can add your own.

- ❏ Thank God for giving each person in your group a story.
- ❏ Thank God for loving you enough to want a relationship with you.
- ❏ Thank God for giving you the skills to listen to friends' stories with compassion and wisdom so you know how their stories might lead to your story or God's story.
- ❏ Thank God for giving you friends who can encourage you to share your story with others.
- ❏ Thank God for friendships and opportunities to share stories with friends.
- ❏ Thank God for living in a country where we can worship him freely.
- ❏ Thank God for your small group leader.

AT HOME THIS WEEK

Daily Bible Readings
Check out the Scriptures on page 108.

Memory Verses
Try memorizing a verse from page 112.

Journaling
Use **SCRIBBLE** pages, 117-125
- Write whatever is on your mind.
- Read your journal entry from last week and write a reflection on it.
- Respond to these questions: *What are some ways that I might be able to transition an ordinary friendship conversation into a spiritual conversation including my story? Which is more important: listening to a friend's story or sharing my story? Why?*

Wrap It Up
Write out your answers to the session questions your group didn't have time to discuss.

LEARN A LITTLE MORE

Background: praying like Paul
Half of the passage you studied is about prayer. It's a spiritual habit that humbles most Christians. Cultivating a consistent prayer life is difficult, and it takes a strong commitment to establish this habit. The greater context of Colossians gives us more insight into Paul's instruction on prayer. To strengthen the church at Colosse, Paul presents strong warnings against deception:

> [4]I tell you this so that no one may deceive you by fine-sounding arguments... [8]See to it that no one takes you captive through hollow and deceptive philosophy, which depends on human tradition and the basic principles of this world rather than on Christ... [18]Do not let anyone who delights in false humility and the worship of angels disqualify you for the prize. Such a person goes into great detail about what he has seen, and his unspiritual mind puffs him up with idle notions.
>
> —Colossians 2:4, 8, 18

Without watchfulness, deception will win. Your prayers help guard your heart and mind against the deceptions of the world. Without thankfulness, prayers are worthless. The heart of your worship to God is expressed with acknowledgment that "God is good" and the humble response of "thanks."

Paul also instructs the church to pray not only for themselves, but also to pray for other believers, specifically for open doors of opportunity and the clear presentation of the gospel. If Paul needed prayer, then so do we!

Background: divine appointments

If God really has the kind of power, love, and wisdom that he claims, we can accept his control over the events and circumstances of our lives. The big churchy phrase for this is *divine providence.* God wants to do great things through your life, making a real and lasting impact on others. God is going to make sure you're in the right place at the right time to make a difference for him. These are divine appointments you don't want to miss. Be wise, learn from your mistakes, see opportunities for what they are, and do the right thing!

Let your conversation be always full of grace

Words are powerful! They can cut deep and leave scars that last a lifetime. Careless jabs can hurt even more than intentional attacks. Our world needs conversations filled with grace. Rather than practicing one-upmanship, offer a compliment. Instead of correcting every little mistake, offer grace and let the mistake pass without correcting it. Consider dropping sarcasm in favor of encouragement. Anyone who offers grace is a breath of fresh air in the world—and it's desperately needed!

FOR FURTHER STUDY

Philippians 1:27-30; 2:14-18
1 Corinthians 4:1-2
1 Peter 2:11-25

NOTES

NOTES

SHARING GOD'S STORY

The title of this session can be intimidating at first glance. A normal response might be, "Explaining God's story? No way. I barely understand it myself."

Many people would rather be kicked in the head than explain what God is all about. Or you might think a better solution is to bring your non-Christian friends to church and have a leader explain God's story.

I understand your fear, I see it in others all the time, and I feel it myself. I admit it! Even for a pastor, trying to explain what God has done can be awkward and scary. Fear will continue to haunt you until you take the opportunity to share what you know about God and what you've personally experienced—your story.

As you build or strengthen friendships and listen to others' stories (look back at session 3 if you want a reminder), you'll have opportunities to explain your story. In session 4, your small group discussed the importance of sharing this story. Sometimes you'll have an opportunity to introduce God's story when you have spiritual conversations. The good news is that you don't have to understand everything about God in order to talk about him with others. No one understands everything about God, not even brilliant people who spend their entire lives studying about God. God's nature and character are mysterious and can't be fully understood by people.

When you share God's story in your spiritual conversations, be honest about your own confusion and some of the hurts and questions you have. The more honest you are, the more appealing your words will be. Also don't get caught up in teaching every detail of God's character and all of his plans for the entire world. Focus on the basics. At the core of the New Testament is Jesus, the God-man who came to seek and save those who are lost. The central message of Jesus is connecting God's creation (people) into his kingdom (family), so they move from the impersonal status of "creation" to the personal relationship of "child." That's why it's called good news. Explain your true need to be rescued and how you really knew you needed a Savior (again part of your story).

God wants everyone to be part of his family, and he took radical measures to open the door of his home. It's quite a story! Your job isn't to convert people. That's God's role. Your task is to be faithful to care about your friend, share your story, and add what you can about God's story. You can do it!

You'll be amazed at what God does in your life when you talk to others about him. Now, as a small group, cheer one another on and encourage the group members to take steps to learn more of God's story.

FELLOWSHIP: CONNECTING Your Heart to Others

Everyone has some fears when it comes to talking about God to non-Christians. In the evangelism section of this session, you'll see how all the stories work together, but before you get there (make sure you don't skip the evangelism section of this session) spend a few moments to talk about your personal reservations.

What fears might you experience if you had to leave the small group right now to tell a friend—who wants to know—about God's story?

 Are any of your fears new? Which ones hadn't you heard of or experienced before?

DISCIPLESHIP: GROWING to Be Like Jesus

Fear can be a good thing. If you're afraid of a wild bear, you're not going to jump into his cage when you're at the zoo. Fear can also be a bad thing—when you fear things you have no need to fear. One of my friends has an irrational fear of cockroaches. He'd rather be in a shark-infested tank than touch a cockroach.

Could sharing God's story possibly be an irrational fear? Peter understood the fear that most of us feel when it comes to sharing our faith with others. His spiritual insight might be just what you need to overcome your fears.

[13]Who is going to harm you if you are eager to do good? [14]But even if you should suffer for what is right, you are blessed. "Do not fear what they fear; do not be frightened." [15]But in your hearts set apart Christ as Lord. Always be prepared to give an answer to everyone who asks you to give the reason for the hope that you have. But do this with gentleness and respect, [16]keeping a clear conscience, so that those who speak maliciously against your good behavior in Christ may be ashamed of their slander. [17]It is better, if it is God's will, to suffer for doing good than for doing evil.

—1 Peter 3:13-17

Why might Peter mention the word **harm?** How does being harmed relate to sharing your story or God's story with others?

When it comes to sharing your faith with others, what kind of tone should you have? What are some key words from this passage that describe the kind of approach to take?

How might fear reflect the condition of your heart?

Why does Peter encourage us to set apart Christ as Lord in our hearts? What does this have to do with sharing our faith?

This passage says, "Do not fear what they fear." What are the kinds of fears unbelievers have that Christians don't need to have? Think specifically about some of your non-Christian friends.

Why do you think being accepted by others holds so much power over the way we live our lives?

7

8

What does it mean to always be ready to answer? Does it mean you should be able to answer any question someone might ask? Explain your thinking.

What do gentleness and respect have to do with sharing your faith?

9

When you consider your own attitude toward unbelievers, would you use the words **gentleness** and **respect?** If not, what words would you use?

10

What does this passage teach about suffering? (You may need to reread these verses to come up with a complete answer.)

11

On the next page are two passages that give the essence of the gospel. Read them as a group. Then explain in your own words the essence of the gospel.

16"For God so loved the world that he gave his one and only Son, that whoever believes in him shall not perish but have eternal life. 17For God did not send his Son into the world to condemn the world, but to save the world through him."

—John 3:16-17

3For what I received I passed on to you as of first importance: that Christ died for our sins according to the Scriptures, 4that he was buried, that he was raised on the third day according to the Scriptures, 5and that he appeared to Peter, and then to the Twelve. 6After that, he appeared to more than five hundred of the brothers at the same time.

—1 Corinthians 15:3-6

MINISTRY: SERVING Others in Love

This is another opportunity to serve those in your small group. The action step of sharing God's story is not only intimidating, but it's tough if you don't know much of God's story.

Have someone (or a few people) make a commitment to find three tools or resources that can help your small group's members know more about God's story. Bring copies of the resources to the next small group meeting. Be committed to doing it, okay? (You may want someone to check in with you during the week to check on your progress.) Now move on to the evangelism section. Don't skip it!

EVANGELISM: SHARING Your Story and God's Story

Read the following paragraphs (they're a little longer than usual) and discuss the answers to the questions that follow.

You can't reduce the wonderful and amazing mysteries of God's story into quick easy steps, a simple drawing, or a fast prayer. Effective evangelism revolves around caring relationships and honest stories. That's what this entire book is about.

As you think about evangelism, I'd like for you to understand how God's story might combine with each of the following to create more powerful spiritual conversations:

- Lifestyle
- Friendships
- Your story
- Their story

Lifestyle

No evangelistic technique (drawing a picture, using verbal tactics, memorizing verses) will mean anything if a friend doesn't believe God's presence has made any difference in your life. Bottom line: your lifestyle plays a supporting role in your evangelism. Remember, Peter said we ought to live good lives and share our answers with gentleness and respect. If friends with whom you share your stroy have no reason to respect you, they won't listen.

Friendships

Sessions 1, 2, and 3 were about developing and deepening friendships. Your story, their story, and God's story make the most sense in the context of genuine friendships. For most people it's difficult to unfold God's love without showing it in the way you treat others. In today's world a friend who listens with understanding and care displays a profound act of love (the foundation of friendship and evangelism).

Your Story

Your friends have their own ideas about God, and they have no reason to assume your ideas are any better informed than theirs. But because of your friendship, they'll most likely be interested in knowing more about you and your faith story.

So you uncover your story as fearlessly as you know how, telling the truth about who you really are and how you really need Jesus (session 4). Depth is better than speed—it may take a while to get the story out. That's okay. The better your friends get to know you (because you're honest about your need for Jesus every day), the clearer it becomes that you're not speaking from a position of moral or spiritual superiority but as someone just like them. It may not be long before it occurs to your friends that, if you need a rescuer (Jesus), they do too.

Their Story

The reason you probably want to start with your story is simply because someone needs to go first or you'll never get your conversation past sports, movies, or music—which are easy to talk about but have no lasting value.

Your friendship and the model of telling your story can make it safe for your friend to uncover their story. As they share their story, the connecting points between your story and their story become obvious. Not because the details of your lives are the same but because your hearts are the same: you hurt like they hurt, you desire what they desire, you've messed up like they've messed up. You're the same in a lot of ways!

Tying It All Together

The connecting points between your stories and your friend's story will give you an idea where God's story might fit in, so the better you know God's story, the easier it will be to know which parts to share. (This is a great reason to learn the Gospels backward and forward). Most non-Christians aren't afraid of Jesus. They're afraid of Christians. Jesus can meet them where they are.

As you keep discovering their story, uncovering your story, and unfolding God's story you can be introducing your non-Christian friend to your Christian friends at school and the community of genuine believers at your church. Then, every so often, like a good farmer, give a gentle tug to see if the fruit is ready to be picked by saying something like, "Is this making sense to you?" or "What do you wish God would tell you?"

When the fruit is ripe, it will come off in your hand; if it's not ripe, don't pull on it. It's not your job to ripen the fruit, just to harvest it when it's ready.

That's a picture of friendship evangelism in a nutshell. No key verses, no tactics, no "pray the prayer." Just connect as much of God's story as you know to as much of their story as you know, all the while being fearlessly honest with your story—with who you really are and how you really need Jesus.

There is nothing magical about this process. It's not like a spiritual connect-the-dots guaranteed to convert everyone. You won't lose any spiritual points if your friend doesn't immediately respond. Relax. Love your friend. Allow the Holy Spirit to do his work. You can be there for questions, for prayer, for friendship, and for acceptance even if your friend doesn't seem ready. Allow your friend time to think, converse, and make sure your friend knows you're always available to talk.

14 What are your thoughts about how all these pieces fit together?

15 How long might a relationship like this take to develop?

16 What do you need to know about God's story?

17 What do you like best about these ideas? Least?

WORSHIP: SURRENDERING Your Life to Honor God

Pray together as a group and have each person choose one of the following feelings to pray for. (It's okay to have them repeated if your small group is larger than five.)

- Acknowledge that you feel unworthy sharing God's story.
- Acknowledge that you feel honored that God would use you.
- Acknowledge that you feel scared.
- Acknowledge that friendships like this can be difficult to form.
- Acknowledge that you may not understand how all the stories fit together.

AT HOME THIS WEEK

Daily Bible Readings
Check out the Scriptures on page 108.

Memory Verses
Try memorizing a verse from page 112.

Journaling
Use **SCRIBBLE** pages, 117-125

- Write whatever is on your mind.
- Read your journal entry from last week and write a reflection on it.
- Respond to these questions: *How can I be real about my life, hurts, fears, and failings as I share my story? Are there any fears that I didn't mention in my small group?* Write about them.

Wrap It Up
Write out your answers to the session questions your group didn't have time to discuss.

LEARN A LITTLE MORE

An answer

A verbal explanation of what you believe. The word literally means "defense," but you don't need to be defensive. Someone can reject your beliefs and not disrupt your confidence since your confidence doesn't rest in what people think of you. Your words come from what the Bible teaches about salvation.

Background: Jesus saves

When you hear that Jesus saves, it means that Jesus' death rescued you from the penalty that's owed for your sin. Sin is rebellion and disobedience against God. The penalty for sin is eternal separation from God. Jesus came to rescue the world from this separation.

Background: Jesus died for our sins

If you burned down someone's house, and the judge both went to jail in your place and paid for the house to be rebuilt, this would be something like what Jesus did on the cross. Your sins are like a crime, requiring a debt you can't pay. The cost is more money than you can make in a lifetime. For God to release you from the debt, someone else has to pay the debt for you. The debt can't simply be ignored, because someone has to pay to rebuild the house. Sin means you have been torching God's property all your life. Even nice, good, and kind people do far more damage than they'd admit. Jesus paid the price to restore what you have harmed and also to restore you to the person you were made to be.

FOR FURTHER STUDY

Proverbs 14:12
John 3:16-21; 10:10
Romans 3:9-18, 21-26; 5:1-2, 6-8

If you are watching the LifeTogether DVD, you may use this page to take notes.

NOTES

If you are watching the LifeTogether DVD, you may use this page to take notes.

JESUS' FINAL WORDS

If I knew that tomorrow was the last day I would ever have to communicate to my children, I would think deeply about what I wanted to say to them. My final words would need to be unforgettable, the real gems from my treasure box of fatherly wisdom. But since I don't have the foreknowledge of when that will be, I tell them every day, "I love you" and then try to act as if it's my last.

Jesus had the privilege of knowing when his last days would be, so he directed some powerful words to his closest friends. He challenged them to reach the world. Since Jesus came to seek and save the lost, it makes sense that he'd want his life mission passed on to those who would relay God's story to others. On two occasions (which you'll study today), Jesus gave similar instructions: "Go and make disciples of all nations" (Matthew 28:19), and "You will receive power and will tell people about me everywhere...to the ends of the earth" (Acts 1:8 NLT). Jesus understood his assignment, and he knew the assignment for his followers: go and tell.

I'm proud of you for persevering through the tough challenges in this book. I applaud any steps you have taken to develop a heart for God's people and a desire to share your story and God's story. It's a crazy thought that God would use us to lead people his way. He doesn't need to use us, but he does—if we're willing.

Finish strongly today. Love one another. Challenge one another. And allow God's Spirit to continue changing you so you can see people as he does. God's blessings on you!

FELLOWSHIP: CONNECTING Your Heart to Others'

1

If you had only one message to leave as part of your life legacy, what would your message be?

2

If today were your last day, what would others say about the message your life has communicated?

DISCIPLESHIP: GROWING to Be Like Jesus

This is the final session for discussing evangelism. It seems appropriate to discuss Jesus' final words recorded in two books of the Bible.

16Then the eleven disciples went to Galilee, to the mountain where Jesus had told them to go. 17When they saw him, they worshiped him; but some doubted. 18Then Jesus came to them and said, "All authority in heaven and on earth has been given to me. 19Therefore go and make disciples of all nations, baptizing them in the name of the Father and of the Son and of the Holy Spirit, 20and teaching them to obey everything I have commanded you. And surely I am with you always, to the very end of the age."
—Matthew 28:16-20

Why does this passage mention the doubt of some of the disciples?

What's so important about authority? Why does Jesus claim to have "all authority"? What clues in the text help answer this question?

Make a list of all of the commands Jesus gives in this passage.

Explain what his commands mean to you in your world today. Take the time to unpack this passage and apply it to your life.

What does it mean to teach others to obey the commands of Jesus?

8

At the end of the passage in Matthew, Jesus promises to be with us until the end of the age; but in this Acts passage, Jesus is taken up to heaven. How can we explain the discrepancy?

9

Jesus promised to send the Holy Spirit to give his disciples power. How has the Holy Spirit helped you recently?

How does the Holy Spirit help us share God's story with others?

10

Why would Jesus leave these statements as his final words to the disciples (and us)?

11

If Jesus spoke these words to you, what would be your response? Your feelings?

MINISTRY: SERVING Others in Love

This entire book is to help you develop a heart for those who don't know God and to give you some ideas on how you might share your story and God's story appropriately and look for connecting points to meet a friend's story. The sessions have been focused on your personal evangelism. But there is more to evangelism and reaching others than merely what you do on your own. Your youth group environment can either assist your evangelistic efforts or hinder them. For example, if a non-Christian student isn't greeted, he doesn't feel like his presence is appreciated. Or if he feels uncomfortable in your youth group, he isn't likely to take interest in God's story or return to your youth group.

What can your youth group do to help create a stronger evangelistic environment and draw unbelievers in?

How can these ideas become part of an evangel-istic interest? Who from your small group can take the lead on these ideas? What will you do? How can others in the group provide support?

EVANGELISM: SHARING Your Story and God's Story

If you had to "make disciples of all nations" on your own, it would be impossible! But that's the point of life together—you depend on the power of the Holy Spirit and you rely on each other.

In your final moments, review the main themes from each lesson. Without looking back through your notes, what do you remember about each discussion?

Session 1: Developing a Heart of Compassion

Session 2: Behind the Mask

Session 3: Building Friendships

Session 4: Sharing Your Story

Session 5: Sharing God's Story

Share the one chapter that you need to review the most or that you need help with the most. Which person in your small group is strongest in that area and can help you?

In Acts 1:8, Jesus tells his followers to be his witness in Jerusalem, Judea, Samaria, and to the ends of the earth. This verse describes a widening circle of influence—local and then expanding throughout the world. How would you describe your circle of influence? Is it increasing? (You'll find more information about the geographic significance of this statement on page 86).

WORSHIP: SURRENDERING Your Life to Honor God

You have two options for your group's closing time.

Review your "no way" list

Go back to your list on page 26 and 27, and comment on any visible signs of God working to bring those people closer to him. You might review what you've done to be part of God's life-changing process. After you discuss this and conclude with your thoughts, feelings, and ideas about evangelism, spend time in prayer, especially for the following three areas:

- The people you named on your lists.
- Your evangelistic efforts (sharing your story; sharing God's story; looking for points of connection with a friend's story).
- Your youth group's friendliness toward people who are new.

Prayer is an essential element of evangelism. It prepares your heart and helps you become sensitive to God's leading. Keep praying for your lost friends, even after you finish this book.

Celebrate with communion

Communion is a way for Christians to remember God's story. Communion is our celebration that reminds us of what Jesus did for us through his death on the cross.

Not every small group can or should take Communion. Some churches require that an ordained minister or priest serve Communion. If that's the case for you (or if you have other theological concerns), the first option is a great way to finish your time together.

www.simplyyouthministries.com/lifetogether

After either option, end your time together by thanking God for what you've learned in this group. Also, be sure to thank your leader for investing time in you.

WHAT'S NEXT?

17 Do you agree to continue meeting together? If yes, continue on with the remaining questions.

Five other books in the LIFETOGETHER series help you establish God's purposes in your life. Discuss which topic your group will study next.

- ☐ **Starting to Go Where God Wants You to Be:** 6 Small Group Sessions on Life Together
- ☐ **Connecting Your Heart to Others:** 6 Small Group Sessions on Fellowship
- ☐ **Growing to Be Like Jesus:** 6 Small Group Sessions on Discipleship
- ☐ **Serving Others in Love:** 6 Small Group Sessions on Ministry
- ☐ **Surrendering Your Life to Honor God:** 6 Small Group Sessions on Worship

18 Turn to the **Small Group Covenant** (page 92). Do you want to change anything in your covenant—time, date, shared values, and so on? Write down the changes you agree upon. (Transfer them into your next LIFETOGETHER book.)

This is a good time to make suggestions for other changes—starting **on time**, paying attention when others are sharing, rotating leadership responsibilities, or whatever ideas you have—for improving the group.

AT HOME THIS WEEK

Daily Bible Readings
Check out the Scriptures on page 108.

Memory Verses
Try memorizing a verse from page 112.

Journaling
Use **SCRIBBLE** pages, 117-125

- Write whatever is on your mind.
- Read your journal entry from last week and write a reflection on it.
- Respond to this question: *If I knew I would die within the next week, what would be my last words to my best friends?*

Wrap It Up
Write out your answers to the session questions your group didn't have time to discuss.

LEARN A LITTLE MORE

Eleven disciples
Jesus originally chose twelve disciples, but after his betrayal, Judas hanged himself. Later another disciple is chosen to bring the number to twelve again. (See Matthew 27:3-5 and Acts 1:21-26.)

All authority
Commands are only worth obeying if they come from a source with sufficient authority. The police officer following you on the freeway has enough authority to command your obedience to the law. Jesus wasn't bashful about his authority. The book of Hebrews gives us a thorough description of the authority of Jesus. Jesus is the exact representation of God (1:3), superior to the angels (1:4) greater than Moses (3:3) or any high priest (chapters 5 and 7). Since Jesus clearly demonstrated his ultimate authority by defeating death, his commandments are to be obeyed.

Teaching them to obey

True learning is much more than the absorption of facts and information and truths. Real learning results in life changes. As Christians who are called to teach others to obey the commands of Christ, we shouldn't just compile a list of essential truths, drill them into others, and get them to repeat that information back. Our goal is always life change. We teach the truth that's necessary for living a life that pleases and honors God.

There are tons of interesting facts in the Bible. Did you know that Jesus once slept on a cushion in a boat in the middle of a lake? He really did. Check out Mark 4:38 if you don't believe me. But personal exploration and explaining these things to others should be secondary to practical truth.

Let's return to the cushion: What was it made of? Was it a boat cushion, or did someone grab it out of a house and bring it for Jesus to use? Did someone tackle Jesus the day before and give him a sore hip? If this happened, do you think Judas was the one who did this? Could this cushion also be considered a pillow or was it really only a cushion? What practical application can we make from Jesus sitting on a cushion? Does thorough study of this historical reality of the cushion do anything to help us obey Jesus better?

Truth that is important is the truth that moves us to live in obedience to Christ. Christians often get caught up in details that hold little significance when it comes to obeying the commands of Jesus.

Jerusalem, and in all Judea and Samaria, and to the ends of the earth

Geography isn't my favorite subject, but a little background information can bring to light the meaning of Jesus' words in this passage. When Jesus made this comment to his disciples, they were standing in the city of Jerusalem. Their witness about Jesus would begin there. Judea was the larger region that surrounded Jerusalem. To translate *Judea* into modern terms, it's comparable to a county.

Samaria was another region, also like a county, that bordered Judea. It's especially significant because of the people who lived there. The Samaritans were culturally and racially different from the Jews. (All of the disciples were Jewish.) You can imagine how surprising these commands from Jesus were: He wanted the disciples to reach out beyond their own culture.

"To the ends of the earth" seems clear enough: Jesus wanted his disciples to share their faith and the truth about the gospel with every nation. Even today, more than 2,000 years after Jesus issued this command, there are still regions of the world that haven't heard the gospel. Because of evangelism, that will one day change.

FOR FURTHER STUDY

Matthew 9:35-38; 10:1-42
Acts 12:25; 13:4-5; 15:36, 41

APPENDIXES

LISTENING LIKE JESUS

With insight from the Holy Spirit, Jesus knew that the Samaritan woman had been married five times. (Review session 2, Discipling, page 35.) The Holy Spirit may not give you such dramatic insight, but he does want to help you understand the real needs of those around you. With practice, prayer, and careful attention you can learn to notice the brokenness people try to hide. Jesus' interaction with the Samaritan woman was a great model of some practical steps to take as you care for the needs of others.

Read this with another person from your small group and discuss what you learn about caring for people and what you might do differently.

Be friendly.
Most people are as thirsty for respect and kindness as the Samaritan woman was.

Ask and answer questions.
Sensitive questions can speak powerfully to people about your respect and concern for them. Consider practicing the following actions with your spiritual partner:

- Rephrase what your partner has shared with you.
- Repeat your partner's last sentence to encourage him or her to share more.
- Return your partner's comment with another question.
- Respond with encouragement for your partner's willingness to share.
- Renew your commitment to listen to and pray for your partner.

Show concern for their needs.
As you listen to the needs others express, it's good to try to feel the emotion they are feeling. You can't fake this. Pray for God's sensitivity as you speak with others. By listening well, you can draw more out from others.

Faithfully explain the Scriptures.
This is where the truth and the power for life change come from. Be prepared to either explain the Scriptures or say, "I'd like to explore your questions in the Bible and get back to you soon," or, "Would you be interested in reading through the Gospel of John with me? We could learn more about Jesus together."

Emphasize the good news to thirsty people.

Remember, your job is to graciously and truthfully share about God's crazy love and what it means to you. The Holy Spirit does the work of converting people. You do the possible with faith that God will do the impossible.

What was the result of Jesus' meeting with the woman at the well? People came streaming from the village to see Jesus. We can reasonably assume the town was never the same again. The same could happen with those from your school.

In John 9 we find an incredible scene: Jesus healed a blind man by restoring his sight. Once healed, the man became a walking testimony of God's strength displayed through Jesus. He experienced a changed life and had a personal story to tell even though he didn't know all the facts about Jesus. He missed most questions asked of him, but he just kept telling how his life had been changed by Jesus: "One thing I do know. I was blind but now I see!" (John 9:26 NIV).

While this specific event reflects physical healing, it's a great illustration of what can happen when you've been spiritually healed. You have a story to share. Read John 9 and the key points below. Either discuss the questions with the group or write answers to the questions on your own. It's good to be prepared with how to respond when you don't know everything.

This man had a story.
What was his story?

The man didn't have all the right answers, but he still had a story.
How does that relate to you and your fears?

The man didn't know everything about Jesus, but he still had a story.
What happens when you don't know everything about Jesus?

The man angered the religious leaders with his story, but he still had a story.
In what ways might your story anger others? If it does, what might you do?

Read through the following covenant as a group. Discuss concerns and questions. You may modify the covenant based on the needs and concerns of your group members. Those who agree with the terms and are willing to commit themselves to the covenant as you've revised it should sign their own books and the books of everyone entering into the covenant.

> A covenant is a binding agreement or contract. God made covenants with Noah, Abraham, and David, among others. Jesus is the fulfillment of a new covenant between God and his people.

If you take your commitment to the Small Group Covenant seriously, you'll find that your group will go deep relationally. Without a covenant you may find yourselves meeting simply for the sake of meeting.

If your group decides to add some additional values (character traits such as be encouraging or be kind), write the new values at the bottom of the covenant page. Your group may also want to create some small group rules (actions such as not interrupting when someone else is speaking or sitting up instead of lying down). You can list those at the bottom of the covenant page also.

Reviewing your group's covenant, values, and rules before each meeting will become a significant part of your small group experience.

OUR COVENANT

I, _____ , as a member of our small group, acknowledge my need for meaningful relationships with other believers. I agree that this small group community exists to help me deepen my relationships with God, Christians, and other people in my life. I commit to the following:

Consistency I will give my best effort to attend every time our small group meets.

Honesty I will take risks to share truthfully about the personal issues in my life.

Confidentiality I will support the foundation of trust in our small group by not participating in gossip. I will not reveal personal information shared by others during our meetings.

Respect I will help create a safe environment for our small group members by listening carefully and not making fun of others.

Prayer I will make a committed effort to pray regularly for the people in our small group.

Accountability I will allow the people in my small group to hold me accountable for growing spiritually and living a life that honors God.

This covenant, signed by all the members in this group, reflects our commitment to one another.

_____   _____
Signature   Date

_____   _____
Signature   Date

_____   _____
Signature   Date

_____   _____
Signature   Date

_____   _____
Signature   Date

_____   _____
Signature   Date

_____   _____
Signature   Date

_____   _____
Signature   Date

_____   _____
Signature   Date

_____   _____
Signature   Date

SMALL GROUP Roster

name	email

SHARING your story and God's story

Phone	AdDress	school & GRADE

HOW TO KEEP YOUR SMALL GROUP FROM BECOMING A CLIQUE

Cliques arise naturally because we all want to belong—God created us to be connected in community with one another. The same drive that creates community creates cliques. A clique isn't just a group of friends, but a group of friends uninterested in anyone outside the group. Cliques result in pain for those who are excluded.

If you reread the first paragraph of the introduction "**Read Me First**" (page 9), you see the words *spiritual community* used to describe your small group. If your small group becomes a clique, it's an *unspiritual* community. You have a clique when the biblical purpose of fellowship turns inward. That's ugly. It's the opposite of what God intended the body of Christ to be.

- Cliques make your youth ministry look bad.
- Cliques make your small group appear immature.
- Cliques hurt the feelings of excluded people.
- Cliques contradict the value God places on each person.
- Few things are as unappealing as a youth ministry filled with cliques.

Many leaders avoid using small groups as a means toward spiritual growth because they fear the groups will become cliquish. But when they're healthy, small groups can improve the well-being, friendliness, and depth of your youth ministry.

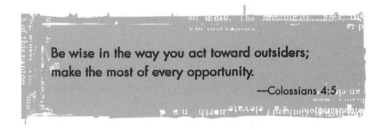

Be wise in the way you act toward outsiders; make the most of every opportunity.

—Colossians 4:5

Here are some ideas for preventing your small group from turning into a clique:

Be Aware

Learn to recognize when people feel like they don't fit in with your group. It's easy to forget when you're an insider how bad it feels to be an outsider.

Reach Out

Once you're aware of a person feeling left out, make efforts to be friendly. Smile, shake hands, say hello, ask them to sit with you or your group, and ask simple yet personalized questions. A person who feels like an outsider may come across as defensive, so be as accepting as possible.

Launch New Small Groups

Any small group that has the attitude of "us four and no more" has become a clique. A time will come when your small group should launch into multiple small groups if it gets too big. The bigger a small group gets, the less healthy it will become. If your small group understands this, there will be a culture of growth instead of cliques. New or introverted people often are affected by cliques because they have a hard time breaking through the existing connections that the small group members already have. When you start new groups you'll see fellowship move from ugly to what God intended—a practical extension of his love.

Challenge Others

Small group members expect adult leaders to confront them for acting like a clique. Instead of waiting for an adult to make the move, shock everyone by stepping up and challenging what you know is destructive. Take a risk. Be a spokesperson for your youth ministry and your student peers by leading the way—be part of a small group that isn't cliquey and one who isn't afraid to challenge the groups who are.

By practicing these key ideas, your group will excel at reaching out to others and deepening the biblical fellowship within your church.

ACCOUNTABILITY QUESTIONS

During your small group time, you'll have opportunities to connect with one other person in the group—your spiritual partner. Relationships can go deeper if you have the same partner for the entire book or even the entire LifeTogether series. Be as mellow as you want or crank it up to a higher level by talking throughout the week and checking in with each other about your spiritual journeys.

For those who want to go to a deeper level with their spiritual partners, here's a list of questions you can use as a guide for accountability. Depending on the time you have available, you might discuss all of them or only a couple.

The Wonder Question
Have you maintained an attitude of awe and wonder toward God?
(Have you minimized him? Placed him in a box? Forgotten to consider his character?)

The Priority Question
Have you maintained a personal devotional time (quiet time) with God?
(Have you allowed yourself to become too busy? Filled your life with too much activity?)

The Morality Question
Have you maintained integrity in the way you live?
(Have you compromised your integrity or the truth with your actions? Your thoughts? Your words?)

The Listening Question
Are you sensitive to the promptings and leading of the Holy Spirit?
(Have you drowned out his voice with too much noise?)

The Relationships Question

Have you maintained peaceful relationships and resolved conflicts to the best of your ability? (Have you caused conflict, offended others, or avoided resolving tension?)

The Prayer Question

How can I pray for you this week?

SPIRITUAL HEALTH assessment

Evaluating your spiritual journey is a good thing. Parts of your journey will take you to low spots, while others will lead you to high places. Spiritual growth is not a smooth incline—loopy roller coaster is more like it. When you regularly consider your life, you'll develop an awareness of God's Spirit working in you. Evaluate. Think. Learn. Grow.

The assessment in this section is a tool, not a test. The purpose of this tool is to help you evaluate where you're at in your faith journey. No one is perfect in this life, so don't worry about what score you get. It won't be published in your church bulletin. Be honest so you have an accurate idea of how you're doing.

When you finish, celebrate the areas where you're relatively healthy, and think about how you can use your strengths to help others on their spiritual journeys. Then think of ways your small group members can aid one another to improve weak areas through support and example.

 FELLOWSHIP: CONNECTING Your Heart to Others'

1. I meet consistently with a small group of Christians.

1	2	3	4	5
poor				outstanding

2. I'm connected to other Christians who hold me accountable.

1	2	3	4	5
poor				outstanding

3. I can talk with my small group leader when I need help, advice, or support.

1	2	3	4	5
poor				outstanding

4. My Christian friends are a significant source of strength and stability in my life.

1	2	3	4	5
poor				outstanding

5. I regularly pray for others in my small group between meetings.

1	2	3	4	5
poor				outstanding

6. I have resolved all conflicts I have had with other Christians and non–Christians.

1	2	3	4	5
poor				outstanding

7. I've done all I possibly can to be a good son or daughter and brother or sister.

1	2	3	4	5
poor				outstanding

Take time to answer the following questions to further evaluate your spiritual health (after your small group meets if you don't have time during the meeting). If you need help with this, schedule a time with your small group leader to talk about your spiritual health.

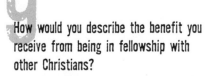

8 List the three most significant relationships you have right now. Why are these people important to you?

9 How would you describe the benefit you receive from being in fellowship with other Christians?

SHARING your story and God's story

Do you have an accountability partner? If so, what have you been doing to hold each other accountable? If not, how can you get one?

DISCIPLESHIP: GROWING to Be Like Jesus

11. I have regular times of conversation with God.

1	2	3	4	5
poor				outstanding

12. I'm a closer friend with God this month than I was last month.

1	2	3	4	5
poor				outstanding

13. I'm making better decisions this month when compared to last month.

1	2	3	4	5
poor				outstanding

14. I regularly attend church services and grow spiritually as a result.

1	2	3	4	5
poor				outstanding

15. I consistently honor God with my finances through giving.

1	2	3	4	5
poor				outstanding

16. I regularly study the Bible on my own.

1	2	3	4	5
poor				outstanding

17. I regularly memorize Bible verses or passages.

1	2	3	4	5
poor				outstanding

Take time to answer the following questions to further evaluate your spiritual health (after your small group meets if you don't have time during the meeting). If you need help with this, schedule a time with your small group leader to talk about your spiritual health.

What books or chapters from the Bible have you read during the last month?

18

19

What has God been teaching you from Scripture lately?

20

What was the last verse you memorized? When did you memorize it? Describe the last time a memorized Bible verse helped you.

MINISTRY: SERVING Others in Love

21. I am currently serving in some ministry capacity.

1	2	3	4	5
poor				outstanding

22. I'm effectively ministering where I'm serving.

1	2	3	4	5
poor				outstanding

23. Generally I have a humble attitude when I serve others.

1	2	3	4	5
poor				outstanding

24. I understand God has created me as a unique individual and he has a special plan for my life.

1   2   3   4   5

poor   outstanding

25. When I help others, I typically don't look for anything in return.

1   2   3   4   5

poor   outstanding

26. My family and friends consider me to be generally unselfish.

1   2   3   4   5

poor   outstanding

27. I'm usually sensitive to the hurts of others and respond in a caring way.

1   2   3   4   5

poor   outstanding

Take time to answer the following questions to further evaluate your spiritual health (after your small group meets if you don't have time during the meeting). If you need help with this, schedule a time with your small group leader to talk about your spiritual health.

If you're currently serving in a ministry, why are you serving? If not, what's kept you from getting involved?

28

29

What spiritual lessons have you learned while serving?

30

What frustrations have you experienced as a result of serving?

31. I regularly pray for my non-Christian friends.

1	2	3	4	5
poor				outstanding

32. I invite my non-Christian friends to church.

1	2	3	4	5
poor				outstanding

33. I talk about my faith with others.

1	2	3	4	5
poor				outstanding

34. I pray for opportunities to share about what Jesus has done in my life.

1	2	3	4	5
poor				outstanding

35. People know I'm a Christian by more than my words.

1	2	3	4	5
poor				outstanding

36. I feel a strong compassion for non-Christians.

1	2	3	4	5
poor				outstanding

37. I have written out my testimony and am ready to share it.

1	2	3	4	5
poor				outstanding

Take time to answer the following questions to further evaluate your spiritual health (after your small group meets if you don't have time during the meeting). If you need help with this, schedule a time with your small group leader to talk about your spiritual health.

Describe any significant spiritual conversations you've had with unbelievers in the past month.

38

Has your faith been challenged by any non–Christians? If yes, how?

39

What have been some difficulties you've faced with sharing your faith?

40

41

What successes have you experienced recently in personal evangelism? (Success isn't limited to bringing people to salvation directly. Helping someone take a step closer at any point on his or her spiritual journey is success.)

WORSHIP: SURRENDERING Your Life to Honor God

42. I consistently participate in Sunday and midweek worship experiences at church.

1	2	3	4	5
poor				outstanding

43. My heart breaks over the things that break God's heart.

1	2	3	4	5
poor				outstanding

44. I regularly give thanks to God.

1	2	3	4	5
poor				outstanding

45. I'm living a life that, overall, honors God.

1	2	3	4	5
poor				outstanding

46. I have an attitude of wonder and awe toward God.

1	2	3	4	5
poor				outstanding

48. I use the free access I have into God's presence often.

1	2	3	4	5
poor				outstanding

Take time to answer the following questions to further evaluate your spiritual health (after your small group meets if you don't have time during the meeting). If you need help with this, schedule a time with your small group leader to talk about your spiritual health.

Make a list of your top five priorities. You can get a good idea of your priorities by evaluating how you spend your time. Be realistic and honest. Are your priorities in the right order? Do you need to

SHARING your story and God's story

get rid of some or add new priorities? (As a student you may have some limitations. This isn't ammo for dropping out of school or disobeying parents!)

50 List ten things you're thankful for.

51 What influences, directs, guides, or controls you the most?

DAILY BIBLE READINGS

As you meet together with your small group friends for Bible study, prayer, and encouragement, you'll grow spiritually. No matter how deep your friendships go, you're not likely to be together for your entire lives, so you need to learn to grow spiritually on your own too. God has given you an incredible tool to help—his love letter, the Bible. The Bible reveals God's love for you and gives directions for living life to the fullest.

To help you, you'll find a collection of Bible passages that reinforce each week's lesson below. Every day *read* the daily verses, *reflect* on how the verses inspire or challenge you, and *respond* to God through prayer or by writing in your journal or on the journaling pages in this book.

Check off the passages as you read them. Don't feel guilty if you miss a daily reading. Simply do your best to develop the habit of being in God's Word daily.

☐ Week 1
Luke 4:38-41
Luke 8:40-56
John 8:1-11
Luke 15:1-10
Luke 15:11-32

☐ Week 2
Luke 19:1-10
Matthew 9:9-12
Acts 9:10-19
Acts 10:34-35
Mark 10:17-25

☐ Week 3
1 Corinthians 3:6-8
2 Corinthians 4:1-6
2 Corinthians 4:7-12
John 4:35-38
Romans 10:13-15

☐ Week 4
John 8:12
John 17:15-19
John 17:20-23
Acts 20:24
John 13:35

☐ Week 5
John 10:10
Romans 3:23
1 Timothy 2:5
Ephesians 2:8-9
John 1:12

☐ Week 6
Acts 1:8
Acts 2:32-39
Acts 17:24-28
1 John 4:7-12
1 John 4:13-18

HOW TO STUDY THE BIBLE

The Bible is the foundation of all the books in the LIFETOGETHER series. Every lesson contains a passage from the Bible for your small group to study and apply. To maximize the impact of your small group experience, it's helpful if each participant spends time reading and studying the Bible during the week. When you read the Bible for yourself, you can have discussions based on what *you* know the Bible says instead of what another member has heard second- or third-hand about the Bible. You also minimize the risk of depending on your small group for all your Bible study time.

Growing Christians learn to study the Bible on their own so they can learn to grow on their own. Here are some principles about studying the Bible to help you give God's Word a central place in your life.

Choose a Time and Place

Since we're so easily distracted, pick a time when you're at your best. If you're a morning person, then give that time to study the Bible. Find a place away from phones, computers, and TVs, so you are less likely to be interrupted.

Begin with Prayer

Make an effort to acknowledge God's presence. Thank him for his gifts, confess your sins, and ask for his guidance and understanding as you study his love letter to you.

Start with Excitement

We easily take God's Word for granted and forget what an incredible gift we have. God wasn't forced to reach out to us, but he did. He's made it possible for us to know him, understand his directions, and be encouraged, all through the Bible. Remind yourself how amazing it is that God wants you to know him.

Read the Passage

After choosing a passage, read it several times. You might want to read it slowly, pausing after each sentence. If possible, read it out loud. Originally the Bible was heard, not read.

Keep a Journal

Respond to God's Word by writing down how you're challenged, truths you want to remember, thanksgiving and praise, sins to confess, commands to obey, or any other thoughts you have.

Dig Deep

When you read the Bible, look deeper than the plain meaning of the words. Here are a few ideas about what you might find.

Truth about God's character
What do the verses reveal about God's character?

Truth about your life and our world
You don't have to figure out life on your own. Life can be difficult, but when you know how the world works you can make good decisions guided by wisdom from God.

Truth about the world's past
The Bible reveals God's intervention in our mistakes and triumphs throughout history. The choices we read about—good and bad—serve as examples to challenge us to greater faith and obedience. (See Hebrews 11:1-12:1.)

Truth about our actions
God will never leave you stranded. Although he allows us to go through hard times, he is always with us. Our actions have consequences and rewards. Just like he does in Bible stories, God can use all of the consequences and rewards caused by our actions to help others.

As you read, ask these four questions to help you learn from the Bible:

What do these verses teach me about who God is, how he acts, and how people respond?

- What does this passage teach about the nature of the world?
- What wisdom can I learn from what I read?
- How should I change my life because of what I learned from these verses?

Ask Questions

You may be tempted to skip over parts you don't understand, but don't give up too easily. Understanding the Bible can be hard work. If you come across a word you don't know, look it up in a regular dictionary or a Bible dictionary. If you come across a verse that seems to contradict another verse, see whether your Bible has any notes to explain it. Write down your questions and ask someone who has more knowledge about the Bible than you. Buy or borrow a study Bible or check the Internet. Try these sites to begin with:

www.twopaths.com
www.gotquestions.org
www.carm.org

Apply the Truth to Your Life

The Bible should make a difference in your life. It contains the help you need to live the life God intended. Knowledge of the Bible without personal obedience is worthless and causes hypocrisy and pride. Take time to consider the condition of your thinking, attitudes, and actions, and wonder about how God is working in you. Think about your life situation and how you can serve others better.

More Helpful Ideas

- Take the position that the times you have set aside for Bible reading and study are nonnegotiable. Don't let other activities squeeze Bible study time out of your schedule.
- Avoid the extremes of being ritualistic (reading a chapter just to mark it off a list) and lazy (giving up).
- Begin with realistic goals and boundaries for your study time. Five to seven minutes a day may be a challenge for you at the beginning.
- Be open to the leading and teaching of God's Spirit.
- Love God like he's your parent (or the parent you wish you had).

MEMORY VERSES

The word *memory* may cause some people to throw this book and kick the dog. Throughout your school years, you have to memorize dates, places, times, and outcomes. Now we're telling you to memorize the Bible?! Seriously?

Not the entire Bible. Start with some key verses. Here's why: Scripture memorization is a good habit for a growing Christian to develop. When God's Word is planted in your mind and heart, it has a way of influencing how you live. King David understood this when he wrote; " I have hidden your word in my heart that I might not sin against you" (Psalm 119:11).

Challenge one another in your small group to memorize the six verses below—one for each time your small group meets. Hold each other accountable by asking about one another's progress. Write the verses on index cards and keep them handy so you can learn and review them when you have free moments (standing in line, before class starts, when you've finished a test and others are still working, waiting for your dad to get out of the bathroom…). You'll be surprised at how many verses you can memorize as you work toward this goal and add verses to your list.

WEEK 1

"For God so loved the world
that he gave his one and only Son,
that whoever believes in him shall not perish
but have eternal life."
—John 3:16

WEEK 2

"For the Son of Man came
to seek and to save
what was lost."
—Luke 19:10

WEEK 3

We are therefore Christ's ambassadors,
as though God were making
his appeal through us.
We implore you on Christ's behalf:
Be reconciled to God.

—2 Corinthians 5:20

WEEK 4

Be wise in the way you act toward outsiders;
make the most of every opportunity.

—Ephesians 2:10

WEEK 5

The Lord is not slow in keeping his promise,
as some understand slowness.
He is patient with you
not wanting anyone to perish,
but everyone to come to repentance.

—2 Peter 3:9

WEEK 6

"Therefore go and make disciples of all nations,
baptising them in the name of the Father
and of the Son and of the Holy spirit,
and teaching them to obey
everything I have commanded you.
And surely I am with you always,
to the very end of the age."

—Matthew 28:19-20

JOURNALING: SNAPSHOTS OF YOUR HEART

In the simplest terms, journaling is reflection with pen in hand. A growing life needs time to reflect, so several times throughout the book you're asked to reflect in writing and you always have a journaling option at the end of each session. Through these writing opportunities, you're getting a taste of what it means to journal.

When you take time to write reflections in a journal, you'll experience many benefits. A journal is more than a diary. It's a series of snapshots of your heart. The goal of journaling is to slow down your life to capture some of the great, crazy, wonderful, chaotic, painful, encouraging, angering, confusing, joyful, and loving thoughts, feelings and ideas that enter your life. Writing in a journal can become a powerful habit when you reflect on your life and how God is working.

You'll find room to journal on the following pages.

Personal Insights

When confusion abounds in your life, disorderly thoughts and feelings can become like wild animals. They often loom just out of range, slightly out of focus, but never gone from your awareness. Putting these thoughts and feelings on paper is like corralling and domesticating the wild beasts. Then you can look at them, consider them, contemplate the reasons they were causing you pain, and learn from them.

Have you ever had trouble answering the question, "How do you feel?" Journaling compels you to become more specific with your generalized thoughts and feelings. This is not to suggest that a page full of words perfectly represents what's happening on the inside. That would be foolish. But journaling can move you closer to understanding more about yourself.

Reflection and Examination

With journaling, once you recognize what you're to write about, you can then consider its value. You can write about your feelings, your situations, how you responded to events. You can reflect and answer questions like these:

- Was that the right response?
- What were my other options?
- Did I lose control and act impulsively?
- If this happened again, should I do the same thing? Would I do the same thing?
- How can I be different as a result of this situation?

Spiritual Insights

One of the main goals of journaling is to learn new spiritual insights about God, yourself, and the world. When you take time to journal, you have the opportunity to pause and consider how God is working in your life and in the lives of those around you, so you don't miss the work he's accomplishing. And journaling helps you remember.

What to Write

There isn't one way to journal, no set number of times per week, no rules for the length of each journal entry. Figure out what works best for you. Get started with these options:

A letter or prayer to God
Many Christians struggle with maintaining a consistent prayer life. Writing out your prayers can help strengthen it. Begin with this question: *What do I want to tell God right now?*

A letter to or a conversation with another person
Sometimes conversations with others can be difficult because we're not sure what we ought to say. Have you ever walked away from an interaction and 20 minutes later think, *I should have said...?* Journaling conversations before they happen can help you think through the issues and be intentional in your interactions with others. As a result, you can feel confident as you begin your conversations because you've taken time to consider the issues.

Conflict and pain
You may find it helpful to write about your conflicts with others, especially those that take you by surprise. By journaling soon after, you can reflect

and learn from the conflicts. You'll be better prepared for the next time you face a similar situation. Conflicts are generally difficult to navigate. Thinking through the interactions typically yields helpful personal insights.

When you're experiencing pain is a good time to settle your thoughts and consider the nature of your feelings. The great thing about exploring your feelings is that you're only accountable to God. You don't have to worry about hurting anyone's feelings by what you write in your journal (if you keep it private).

Personal motivation

The Bible is clear regarding two heart truths:

■ How you act is a reflection of who you are on the inside (Luke 6:45).
■ You can take the right action for the wrong reason (James 4:3).

The condition of your heart is so important. Molding your motives to God's desire is central to being a follower of Christ. The Pharisees did many of the right things, but for the wrong reasons. Reflect on the *real* reasons you do what you do.

Personal Impact

Have you ever gone to bed thinking, *That was a mistake. I didn't intend for that to happen!?* Probably! No one is perfect. You can't predict all of the consequences of your actions. Reflecting on how your actions impact others will help you relate better to others.

God's work in your life

If you write in your journal in the evening, you can answer this question: *What did God teach me today?*

If you journal in the morning, you can answer this question: *God, what were you trying to teach me yesterday that I missed?* When you reflect on yesterday's events, you may find a common theme that God may have been weaving into your life during the day, one you missed because you were busy. When you see God's hand in your life, even a day later, you know God loves you and is guiding you.

Scripture

Journal about whatever you learn from the Bible. Rewrite a verse in your own words, or figure out how a passage is structured. Try to uncover the key truths from the verses and figure out how the verses apply to your life.

SCRIBBLES

SCRIBBLES

JOURNA

SCRIBBLES

SCRIBBLES

SCRIBBLES

SCRIBBLES

sCRIBBLES

SCRIBBLES

rl
rn
le
lu
th
- St. Bernard, and Mount Po
din., and Mount Po
sq. 8,749. The gorming its area, 10

PRAYING IN YOUR SMALL GROUP

A s believers, we're called to support one another in prayer, and prayer should become a consistent part of creating a healthy small group.

One of the purposes of prayer is to align our hearts with God's. By doing this, we can more easily think his thoughts and feel his feelings—in our limited human way. Prayer shouldn't be a how-well-did-I-do performance or a self-conscious, put-on-the-spot task to fear. Your small group may need time to get comfortable with praying out loud. That's okay.

Follow Jesus' Example

When you do pray, silently or aloud, follow the practical, simple words of Jesus in Matthew 6.

Pray sincerely.

"And when you pray, do not be like the hypocrites, for they love to pray standing in the synagogues and on the street corners to be seen by men. I tell you the truth, they have received their reward in full."

—Matthew 6:5

In the Old Testament, God's people were disciplined prayer warriors. They developed specific prayers to use for every special occasion or need. They had prayers for light and darkness, prayers for fire and rain, prayers for good news and bad. They even had prayers for travel, holidays, holy days, and Sabbath days.

Every day the faithful would stop to pray at 9:00 A.M., noon, and 3:00 P.M., a sort of religious coffee break. Their ritual was impressive, to say the least, but being legalistic has its downside. The proud, self-righteous types would strategically plan their schedules to be in the middle of a crowd when it was time for prayer so everyone could hear them as they prayed loudly. You can see the problem. What was intended to promote spiritual passion became a drama for the crowd.

The Lord wants our prayers addressed to him alone. That seems obvious enough, yet how many of us pray more with the need to impress our listeners than to communicate with God? This is the problem if you're prideful like the Pharisees about the excellent quality of your prayers. But it can also be a problem if you're new to prayer and concerned that you don't know how to "pray right." Don't concern yourself with what others think; just talk to God as if you were sitting in a chair next to him.

Pray simply.

"And when you pray, do not keep on babbling like pagans, for they think they will be heard because of their many words. Do not be like them, for your Father knows what you need before you ask him."

—Matthew 6:7-8

The Lord doesn't ask to be dazzled with brilliantly crafted language. Nor is he impressed with lengthy monologues. It's freeing to know that he wants us to keep it simple.

Pray specifically.

"This, then, is how you should pray: 'Our Father in heaven, hallowed be your name, your kingdom come, your will be done on earth as it is in heaven. Give us today our daily bread. Forgive us our debts, as we also have forgiven our debtors. And lead us not into temptation, but deliver us from the evil one."

—Matthew 6:9-13

What the church has come to call **The Lord's Prayer** is a model of the kind of brief but specific prayers we may offer anytime, anywhere. Look at some of the specific items mentioned:

Adoration—hallowed be your name

Provision—your kingdom come...your will be done...give us today our daily bread

Forgiveness—forgive us our debts

Protection—lead us not into temptation

PRAYER REQUEST GUIDELINES

Because prayer time is so vital, small group members need to know some basic guidelines for sharing, handling, and praying for prayer requests. Without a commitment from each person to honor these simple suggestions, prayer time can be dominated by one person, be a gossipfest, or be a never-ending story time. (There are appropriate times to tell personal stories, but this may not be the best time.)

Here are a few suggestions for each group to consider:

Write the requests down.

Each small group member should write down every prayer request on the **Prayer Request Log** (pages 132-137). When you commit to a small group, you're agreeing to be part of the spiritual community, which includes praying for one another. By keeping track of prayer requests, you can be aware of how God answers them. You'll be amazed at God's power and faithfulness.

As an alternative, one person can record the requests and e-mail them to the rest of the group. If your group chooses this option, *safeguard confidentiality.* Be sure personal information isn't compromised. Some people share e-mail accounts with parents or siblings. Develop a workable plan for this option.

Give everyone an opportunity to share.

As a group, be mindful of the amount of time remaining and the number of people who still want to share. You won't be able to share every thought or detail about a situation.

Obviously if someone experiences a crisis, you may need to focus exclusively on that group member by giving him or her extended time and focused prayer. (However, *true* crises are infrequent.)

The leader can limit the time by making a comment such as one of the following:

- Everyone can share one praise or request.
- Simply tell us what to pray for. We can talk more later.
- We're only going to pray for requests about the people in our group.
- We've run out of time to share prayer requests. Take a moment to write down your prayer request and give it to me [or identify another person]. You'll get them by e-mail tomorrow.

Just as people are free to share, they're free to not share.

The goal of a healthy small group should be to create an environment where participants feel comfortable sharing about their lives. Still, not everyone needs to share each week. Here's what I tell my small group:

> As a small group we're here to support one another in prayer. This doesn't mean that everyone has to share something. In fact, I don't want you to think, *I've got to share something.* There's no need to make up prayer requests just to have something to say. If you have something you'd like the group to pray for, let us know. If not, that's fine too.

No gossip allowed.

Don't allow sharing prayer requests to become an excuse for gossip. This is easy to do if you all aren't careful. If you're not part of the problem or solution, consider the information gossip. Sharing the request without the story behind it helps prevent gossip. Also speak in general terms without giving names or details ("I have a friend who's in trouble. God knows who it is. Pray for me that I can be a good friend.").

If a prayer request starts going astray, someone should kindly intercede, perhaps with a question such as, "How can we pray for *you* in this situation?"

Don't give advice or try to fix the problem.

When people share their struggles and problems, a common response is to try to fix the problem by offering advice. At the right time, the group might provide input on a particular problem, but during prayer time, keep focused on praying for the need. Often God's best work in a person's life comes through times of struggle and pain.

Keep in touch.

Make sure you exchange phone numbers and emails before you leave the first meeting, so you can contact someone who needs prayer or encouragement before the next time your group meets. You can write each person's contact information on the **Small Group Roster** (page 94).

During the Small Group Gathering

- One person closes in prayer for the entire group.
- Pray silently. Have one person close the silent prayer time after a while with *Amen.*
- The leader or other group member prays out loud for each person in the group.
- Everyone prays for one request or person. This can be done randomly during prayer or, as the request is shared, a willing pray-er can announce, "I'll pray for that."
- Everyone who wants to pray takes a turn or two. Not everyone needs to pray out loud.
- Split the group into half and pray together in a smaller group.
- Pair up and pray for each other.
- On occasion, each person can share what he or she is thankful for before a prayer request, so prayer requests don't become negative from focusing only on problems. Prayer isn't just asking for stuff. It includes praising God and being thankful for his generosity toward us.

■ If you're having an animated discussion about a Bible passage or a life situation, don't feel like you *must* cut it short for prayer requests. Use it as an opportunity to add a little variety to the prayer time by praying some *other* day between sessions.

Outside the Group Time

You can use these options if you run out of time to pray during the meeting or in addition to prayer during the meeting.

■ Send prayer requests to each other via e-mail.

■ Pick partners and phone each other.

■ Have each person in the small group choose a day to pray for everyone in the group. Perhaps you can work it out to have each day of the week covered. Let participants report back at each meeting for accountability.

■ Have each person pray for just one other person in the group for the entire week. (Everyone prays for the person on the left or on the right or draw names.)

PRAYER REQUEST LOG

DATE	who shared	ReQuest	r8sponse/ anSweR

PRAYER REQUEST LOG

DATE	who shared	ReQuest	r&sponse/ anSweR

PRAYER REQUEST LOG

DATE	who shared	ReQuest	rEsponse/ anSweR

PRAYER REQUEST LOG

DATE	who shared	ReQuest	rEsponse/ anSweR

PRAYER REQUEST LOG

DATE	who shared	ReQuest	rEsponse/anSweR

PRAYER REQUEST LOG

DATE	who shared	ReQuest	response/ anSweR

LIFE TOGETHER FOR A YEAR

Your group will benefit the most if you work through the entire LIFETOGETHER series. The longer your group is together, the better your chances of maturing spiritually and integrating the biblical purposes into your life. Here's a plan to complete the series in one year.

I recommend you begin with **STARTING to Go Where God Wants You to Be**, because it contains an introduction to each of the five biblical purposes (though it isn't mandatory). You can use the rest of the books in any order.

As you look at your youth ministry calendar, you may want to use the books in the order they complement events the youth group will be participating in. For example, if you plan to have an evangelism outreach in the fall, study **SHARING Your Story and God's Story** first to build momentum. Study **SERVING Others in Love** in late winter to prepare for the spring break missions' trip.

Use your imagination to celebrate the completion of each book. Have a worship service, an outreach party, a service project, a fun night out, a meet-the-family dinner, or whatever else you can dream up.

Number of weeks	Meeting topic
1	Planning meeting—a casual gathering to get acquainted, discuss expectations, and refine the covenant (see page 88).
6	**STARTING to Go Where God Wants You to Be**
1	Celebration
6	**CONNECTING Your Heart to Others'**
1	Celebration
6	**SHARING Your Story and God's Story**
1	Celebration
6	**GROWING to Be Like Jesus**
1	Celebration
6	**SERVING Others in Love**
1	Celebration
6	**SURRENDERING Your Life to Honor God**
1	Celebration
2	Christmas break
1	Easter break
6	Summer break
52	One year

Dear Kathleen,

I just wanted to let you know how thankful I am for the dedication you showed me as my small group leader. I love telling people, "Kathleen is my small group leader — she's the best!" Next to God, you have had the greatest influence in my life. I want to grow up and love people like you, love Jesus like you do, love my future husband like you do, and be a small group leader like you.

What's amazing about you, is that all the girls in our small group felt like you liked them the most. We also felt your push. As I look back over my junior high and high school years, you loved me enough to challenge me to change. Thank you for always asking about my prayer life, my quiet times, my ministry, my heart. Thanks for seeing who I could be.

You've made a huge difference in my life. Thank you!

Love,
Sarah

Whether you are a student or a leader, when you're a part of a small group — investing your life in others — you're making a difference that will last an eternity. At Simply Youth Ministry we are dedicated to helping you do just that. For students, we've got tools like the *One Minute Bible*, that will help you grow in your faith. For leaders, we've got all kinds of resources that will help you simplify your ministry and save you time. For both of you, we have a deep appreciation for your commitment to serving Christ and loving each other.

doug fields'
simply youth ministry
simplifying ministry...saving you time.

toll free: 1-866-9-simply
simplyyouthministry.com

ABOUT THE AUTHORS

Doug Fields, a respected youth ministry leader for over two decades, has authored or coauthored more than 30 books, including **Purpose-Driven Youth Ministry, Your First Two Years of Youth Ministry**, and **Videos That Teach**. With an M.Div. from Fuller Theological Seminary, Doug is the youth pastor at Saddleback Church, president of simplyyouthministry.com, and a frequent presenter at Youth Specialties events. Doug and his wife, Cathy, have three children.

Brett Eastman is pastor of membership and small groups at Saddleback Church, where there are now over 1,500 small group leaders and a growing network of volunteer coaches and bivocational pastors. Brett created the Healthy Small Group strategy and he leads the Large Church Small Group Forums for the Leadership Network. Brett is coauthor of the DOING LIFE TOGETHER Bible study series. Brett and his wife, Dee, have five children.